D1593974

Enchanted
Herbal

GAIL BUSSI

first discovered green magic as a little girl in her mother's flower garden. After some years spent writing, designing, and working as a professional cook, she decided to return to her first love and obtained qualifications in holistic herbalism, flower therapies, and mindfulness coaching. Today she lives in a small log cabin on the beautiful Eastern Cape coast of South Africa, where she continues to write, teach, and create natural enchantment every day.

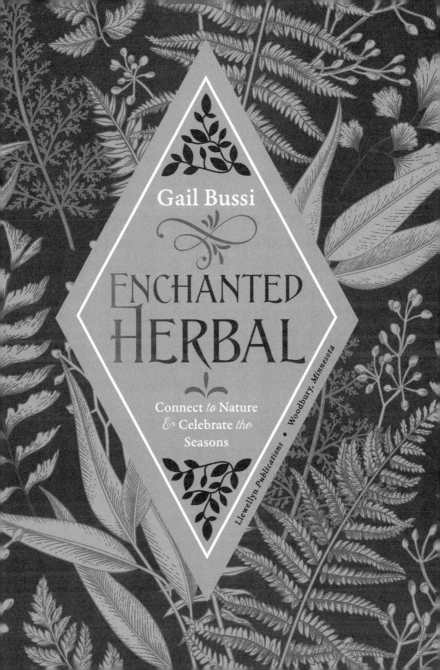

Gail Bussi

ENCHANTED HERBAL

Connect *to* Nature
& Celebrate *the*
Seasons

Llewellyn Publications ● Woodbury, Minnesota

FIRST EDITION
First Printing, 2020

Book design by Rebecca Zins
Cover design by Shira Atakpu

Llewellyn is a registered trademark of Llewellyn Worldwide Ltd.

Library of Congress Cataloging-In-Publication Data
Names: Bussi, Gail, author.
Title: Enchanted herbal : connect to nature and celebrate the seasons /
   Gail Bussi.
Description: First edition. | Woodbury, Minnesota : Llewellyn Publications,
   [2020] | Includes bibliographical references. | Summary: "Written around
   the natural rhythm of the year, *Enchanted Herbal* helps you use each
   season's herbs and flowers to their fullest potential, guiding you to
   become a more magical and joyful person"—Provided by publisher.
Identifiers: LCCN 2020036038 (print) | LCCN 2020036039 (ebook) | ISBN
   9780738766119 (paperback) | ISBN 9780738766591 (ebook)
Subjects: LCSH: Herbs—Miscellanea. | Seasons—Miscellanea.
Classification: LCC BF1623.P5 B87 2020 (print) | LCC BF1623.P5 (ebook) |
   DDC 133/.258—dc23
LC record available at https://lccn.loc.gov/2020036038
LC ebook record available at https://lccn.loc.gov/2020036039

Llewellyn Worldwide Ltd. does not participate in, endorse, or have any authority or responsibility concerning private business transactions between our authors and the public.

All mail addressed to the author is forwarded but the publisher cannot, unless specifically instructed by the author, give out an address or phone number.

Any internet references contained in this work are current at publication time, but the publisher cannot guarantee that a specific location will continue to be maintained. Please refer to the publisher's website for links to authors' websites and other sources.

Llewellyn Publications
A Division of Llewellyn Worldwide Ltd.
2143 Wooddale Drive
Woodbury, MN 55125-2989
www.llewellyn.com
Printed in the United States of America

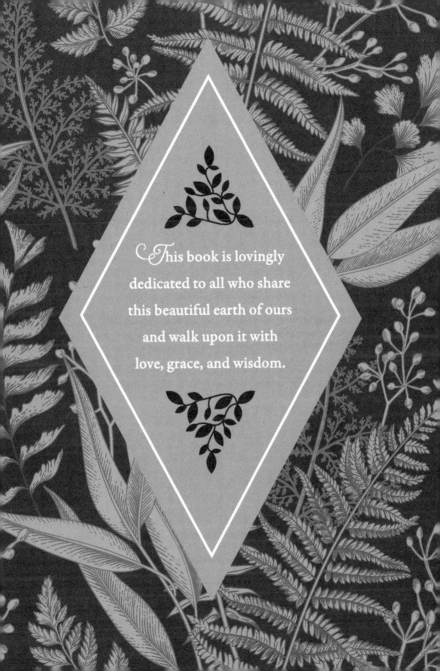

This book is lovingly
dedicated to all who share
this beautiful earth of ours
and walk upon it with
love, grace, and wisdom.

CONTENTS

RECIPES

Things to Eat

Things to Drink

Things to Do

Body Care

Happy Home

INTRODUCTION

In ancient beliefs, alchemy was defined as the art of taking base metals and turning them into pure gold. But I believe we have a simpler and accessible kind of alchemy available to us, whoever and wherever we are. Green alchemy taps into the natural world and its power to transform our "base metals" of fear, illness, anger, loss, and stress into the "gold" that is our true selves. Living an enchanted herbal life gives us a gentle door into that golden and serene place; it also reminds us that not only do we have a duty to support and nurture the world around us in all its forms, but it's vitally important that we nurture ourselves at the same time. Self-care is vital for all of us. Without a true sense of love for ourselves, we cannot be fully present to others and life itself, whether it be human, plant, or animal. Authenticity is the way we become healthy and whole, and in turn we can then offer ourselves and our lives as a true gift to all around us, without fear or self-doubt.

The concept of herbalism means many different things to different people, depending on one's background, spiritual outlook and beliefs, and much more. Medically based herbalism is, obviously, a way of healing ailments of body and spirit using natural remedies and plant energies; when I talk about magic or enchanted herbalism, though, it can lead to confusion, and often people have queried me as to what exactly that means.

Quite simply, I believe magic herbalism uses the unique energies of the plants, herbs, flowers, and trees all around us to help us on every possible level, not just the physical, important though that is. And the opportunities for enchanted herbalism are limitless: we can find them in every moment of the day—in the kitchen, bathroom, garden, or just out on a quiet walk in the woods. There is literally no end to what we can create, grow, harvest, or nurture in a simple and heartfelt way if we are open to the magic that surrounds us and willing to work with it. I would love for you to join me on this beautiful seasonal journey, whoever and wherever you are. Come just as you are. The

earth is waiting for you with her gifts, her warmth, and her unconditional love and acceptance.

I grew up in the 1960s and was definitely a flower child from the start; I could spend hours in my mother's beautiful rose garden or under the indigo African sky, drinking in the intoxicating scent of the pale night-blooming jasmine. (Perhaps even then I already sensed the path I would someday follow.) Today I am sometimes asked if I am a green witch, and although I dislike labels, considering them limiting and oftentimes judgmental, that's one I am happy to wear with both joy and pride. I prefer the term "hearth witch," which I first came across several years ago when I lived in England. It relates to anyone who lives a life close to the earth and her natural gifts and who also uses these gifts in the home to create delicious foods, healing products, and other traditional green magic. I think being a green witch is probably one of the best and most sacred callings anyone can have, as well as being one of total enchantment on every level.

Like many of us, though, my adult life was largely determined by work realities and family routines, and I spent several years living in different countries; then, a few years ago, life decided to give me a fairly big wake-up call. I lost several people very close to me, as well as experiencing a

few other traumatic events. But the road always takes us to a place we need to be, and looking back I realize I was being replanted, given a chance to grow again in a new, richer, and more abundant soil for heart, soul, and body.

For me, this new journey took the form of studying holistic herbalism and flower therapies—both subjects that had long fascinated me. I moved to a small town on the ocean and live in a log cabin in the middle of a forest, surrounded by small lakes, trees, and endless birdsong. Today I write, paint, and create around my central focus of simple natural living and herbal/flower magic. And I am reminded every day, once again, of what I first knew as a little girl looking for ladybugs in my mother's rose garden: life on this earth is both beautiful and fragile, and it is also our greatest and most precious gift, so we need to embrace it fully as we are, where we are, every single day.

I believe that our Mother Earth gives us the gift of life in so many amazing and wonderful forms, but only when we truly seek and embrace these gifts do we find true enchantment. Grace. Growth. Letting go. Health. Possibility. Creation. Hidden deep within our hearts and souls, we have an ancient knowledge and wisdom of this magic, although sometimes life, with its many twists and turns, may take us a step away from the green mysteries. But they never forget

us and wait patiently for our return to the garden, the garden of the heart, so that we may rediscover the joy, innocence, and light we have always carried within and never actually lost.

How to Use This Book

Enchanted Herbal was written around the natural rhythm of the year with its changing seasons, which are so very closely linked to our own journeys, both physical and spiritual. Each season brings its own gifts, lessons, opportunities, and sometimes challenges—but I believe nature also offers us the remedy for these challenges if we are open to connecting with her each and every day of the year.

Each section thus focuses on particular lessons, ideas, and emotions linked to that particular season. Of course, this is not prescriptive: you might have different feelings that come up with the seasons, possibly as a result of past experiences or your own personality. That's why I would encourage you to use this book as a stepping-stone for your own natural magic adventures—and why I also recommend (several times!) keeping different journals or records of your path through the year since you will undoubtedly come up with your own rituals, recipes, and celebrations to remember and cherish!

SPRING: creation and renewal

SUMMER: abundance and passion

AUTUMN: celebration and harvest

WINTER: peace and reflection

Each seasonal chapter encompasses the following sections:

HEART NOTES: thoughts and simple rituals and magic for each season's rhythm

CREATE: simple body/beauty products to make, as well as ideas for a natural home

NURTURE: ideas for natural health and well-being on every level, both physical and spiritual

GROW: practical inspiration for planting, growing, and harvesting one's own herbs and other aromatic plants, and other ideas for garden magic and enchantment

TASTE: seasonal recipes using herbs, spices, and flowers in delicious ways

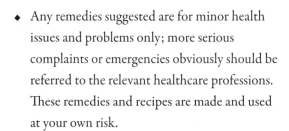

A Few Points to Note

- Any remedies suggested are for minor health issues and problems only; more serious complaints or emergencies obviously should be referred to the relevant healthcare professions. These remedies and recipes are made and used at your own risk.

- Particular caution should be exercised when making and using herb and flower products for use by pregnant/breastfeeding women, as well as babies and very young children. Again, check with your doctor or midwife before using such products, particularly those containing essential oils, some of which should not be used during pregnancy. These include but are not limited to peppermint, cinnamon, juniper, rosemary, oregano, cedarwood, thyme, clove, and sage oils.

- If you have sensitive skin issues or allergies of any kind, it's wise to do a small skin test for twenty-four hours before using homemade skin products, especially those containing essential oils. Apply a small amount and if redness, itching, or irritation develops, do not use that particular remedy.

◆ Some essential oils are photosensitive and should not be applied to skin before spending time in the sun; this includes citrus oils and bergamot.

◆ Essential oils should never be taken internally unless recommended by a medical practitioner and done under supervision.

◆ The recipes and remedies in this book are largely made of a simple range of herbs and basic ingredients that one is likely to have in one's kitchen or store cupboard (although you might need to buy some essential oils). I believe in practical magic and *not* having to buy a whole lot of esoteric (and expensive) ingredients.

◆ Growing your own herbs is a beautiful part of this enchanted journey, even if you have limited space, as I do. Fortunately, I live where there are several organic and farmer's markets so I can generally buy the fresh herbs I cannot grow, as well as the spices and other ingredients I need. I prefer using fresh herbs in general, but sometimes

8

dried herbs are a necessity, depending on the time of year. Some herbs like parsley, chives, and cilantro don't dry well and often end up resembling nothing so much as green dust, with about as much flavor or nutritional value! Others work very well dried—sage, rosemary, and bay leaves, for example—and retain their flavor and color well; however, they should always be kept in glass jars in a cool and dry environment and be replaced at least every six months or so.

Keeping Your Own Green Alchemy Journal

The book you are holding in your hands started out as my own personal green magic journal, a handwritten and illustrated way of recording recipes, ideas, experiments, and insights gained as I followed the path of herbal enchantment through the seasons of the year. It is an invaluable tool that I treasure and add to frequently, and I would like to encourage you to do the same as a unique record of your own.

The whole path of green alchemy is both an intuitive and highly personal one—for example, a fragrance blend that smells wonderful to one person might not appeal at

all to another, and it's often only by trial and error that we discover the best ways of creating our own green path and connections.

You can, of course, choose any journal or notebook that appeals to you—my journal is a large ring-bound book with strong covers and fairly thick ivory pages. (I chose this because I also like to illustrate my journal with little pen and watercolor sketches, so I need paper that will not warp or buckle.) You might be happy with something smaller or even a simple school exercise book; it's entirely a matter of personal taste, and whether you illustrate your journal or not is also up to you. I would, however, suggest sticking a large envelope into the back cover of your notebook or journal, as you will almost certainly find clippings, recipes, or images that you want to cut out and keep, and this makes a perfect place to store them.

On this subject, I suppose it would be possible to keep an online journal in the same way—and if that works for you, go for it! I am a little old-fashioned, I guess, and still prefer something I can physically hold in my hand.

Dating the pages of your green journal is obviously the way to give it structure and serves as an ongoing reminder of what you did and saw, and when. If you are highly organized, unlike me, you might even divide your journal into sections for herbal recipes, health and beauty potions,

garden ideas, and so on. I also suggest carrying a smaller notebook with you when you are spending time outdoors, in your garden and further afield, and use it to record things you see and discover, new plants and wildlife, sights and sounds, emotions and feelings...At a later stage, you can transfer some of these notes into your main garden journal.

SPRING

Creation & Renewal

After the long, dark months of winter, the coming of spring covers the earth with new and abundant life. It reminds us of the renewal we can experience in our own individual lives as we plant seeds of new dreams and visions, then cultivate them. The benefits are not just for ourselves but also for those with whom we share our lives and the greater community that is our earth family.

But growth can only happen when we are open to it, when we make a space for it. After all, we don't throw seeds

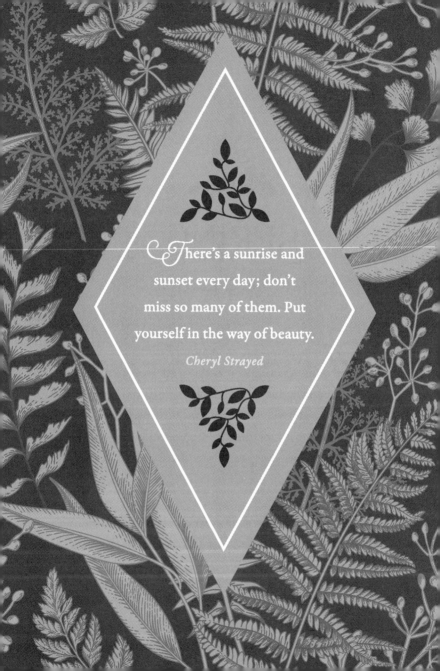

There's a sunrise and sunset every day; don't miss so many of them. Put yourself in the way of beauty.

Cheryl Strayed

onto an already crowded flower bed and hope for the best; no, we carefully clear the space, making sure the seeds will be in the most suitable and fertile spot to grow abundant and strong. We ensure the ground is fertile, and we feed and water the tiny new plants with diligence and love. So it is with our lives—we need to ensure we have cleared away any old, tangled, and unhelpful aspects of our lives that might be creating problems or limitations for us, either physical, mental, or spiritual; only then can we step with clarity and joy into a new spring for both ourselves and the world around us.

Spring offers us a unique opportunity to start fresh and move into our best and healthiest selves. That's one of the reasons I don't make New Year's resolutions—the spring seems a far more appropriate time for such resolves.

HEART NOTES

*G*rowth is all around us in spring, both without and within. In this section you will find a few simple ideas for grounding and growing your heart and spirit during this most fertile and creative of seasons!

Three Candles Ritual

Although this simple ritual can be used all year round, it somehow seems particularly appropriate in springtime. Choose a window that faces the sunrise, and gather together three candles: one pink, one yellow, and one white. I prefer to use fairly large pillar candles as they last longer and make a nice display; the candles can be unscented or you can place a few drops of favorite essential oils in the hollow around the wick. Arrange the candles on a suitable glass or pottery dish; you can also twine some spring flowers and leaves around their bases.

As the sun rises, light the candles and stand or sit in front of them, absorbing both their gentle light and the natural light coming up over the horizon. Then quietly say the following:

> *Pink candle: you remind me of what is in my past, both good and bad—the many lessons learned and gifts received. Thank you.*
>
> *Yellow candle: like the sun, you bless and light this present moment with your grace and warmth; may I never forget my own light within. Thank you.*
>
> *White candle: your pure light scatters any darkness or doubt from the path I have yet to walk into the future. I know I will be kept safe by my mother the earth as I travel with joy and hope in my heart. Thank you.*

You can repeat this ritual as often as you like; I suggest at least once a week, on either a Sunday or Monday morning. This is one of my favorite rituals and one which I think can truly bring about a major shift in attitude on a weekly basis. It's perfectly fine if you want to do it more

often, too! I also find children like a simplified version of this, especially at the beginning of the school week or when they have been having difficulties. Sunrise and sunset are particularly powerful times for us, especially the time just before and after the sun comes up, when it is said we are at our most receptive to spirit and magic.

Spring Cleaning (Inside and Out)

Spring cleaning is an age-old tradition, undoubtedly started to create a brighter and fresher atmosphere after the long, dark, and cold months of winter. Even if it seems a bit of a chore to begin with, ultimately the results are wonderful when we see our surroundings transformed and pleasing to the eye.

But spring cleaning is also an inside job, so to speak—the mind and heart need to be in tune before the true work of decluttering can begin! I am something of a hoarder—I tend to hang on to things like books, magazines, photos, old greeting cards, and other bits and pieces for years, long past it being useful. I know things are piling up and causing me stress, but it always seemed to be just too much of an undertaking to deal with it all. As the Japanese tidying guru Marie Kondo would say, many of these things certainly did not spark joy in me—sometimes exactly the opposite, in

18

fact. For me, as is probably true for many of us, much of my clutter actually brought up painful or best-forgotten memories, such as the pile of emails I kept from a long and abusive relationship.

This short section does not claim to be a practical decluttering guide; there are plenty of those on the market these days. Rather, it's an invitation to look at what we keep and what we choose (or need to) let go of, and why. This spring season, take time to sit quietly and truly think about what it is you really need and want to have in your heart and your life, right here, today. What serves you well…and what no longer does or possibly never did?

Before you actually start the process of cleaning and clearing, I suggest using the magic home cleaning spray (recipe on page 31); you can also burn dried sage or a few sticks of your favorite incense. If you can find them, sprays of lemon verbena leaves arranged in a jug or vase are known to clear and unblock stagnant or bad energies. A bowl of salt or sea water is also useful for removing unwelcome energy in a living or working space. It also helps to walk around the edges of a room you intend to clear and sprinkle a little salt water in each corner; you can also use the smudging bowl blessing ideas in the winter chapter before or after tidying up. This ensures a space that is both blessed and cleansed in every sense of the words.

I have found cleaning and clearing away my accumulated stuff one of the quickest and most positive ways of reducing high stress and anxiety levels. The simpler life is always the most green and enchanted one, one where we can focus on who we are and what we do that matters in the world, rather than focusing on what we possess! The simplified life is generally the happiest life—free on every level, free to be ourselves without added weight and baggage.

The Gifts of Willow

Willow (*Salix alba*) is a graceful and flexible tree; with her flowing, pale green branches she makes the perfect symbol of spring. She is linked to the moon and feminine energy and has been a symbol of protection, healing, and serenity since ancient times. If you are fortunate enough to live close to willow trees, why not spend some time sitting with them and absorbing their gentle strength and quiet lessons?

Willow reminds us to move through the seasons and inevitable changes in our lives with the grace and fluidity of water. We can choose not to become caught up in drama and negativity, especially when it comes to the emotions of others. I am not suggesting we need to be unkind or unsupportive, but we do need to learn when to step back and allow ourselves to simply be, without reaction or stress.

This can be a difficult lesson for many of us, especially us women and empaths in general, but it's a necessary step on the path to wholeness and true freedom. Moving away from rigid and unhelpful thought patterns is the first step on the journey to becoming our true, free selves.

Willow is one of the Bach flower remedies and as such is linked to the soul qualities of personal growth and constructive action instead of becoming stuck in negative and resentful thinking, blaming others or the world at large for the fact we can't have, do, or be what we want. Rather, we can learn to accept any choices we have made in the past that did not serve us, while now taking personal responsibility for making new and better choices for ourselves, giving us the grace to grow supple and strong like the beautiful willow.

Keeping a Moon Magic Journal

Few of us can be unaware of the benefits to be found in keeping a personal journal—a companion and a source of insight, focus, and creative renewal. Obviously, people keep different kinds of journals for very individual reasons, but this spring I am going to suggest beginning a creative journal specifically linked to the moon, which is the source of much creative power for us. I have a beautiful small journal with a silver cover that I keep for this purpose. It is tied

up with a purple ribbon to which I have added small silver charms, rose quartz and citrine crystals, and a few seashells. Just picking up this book brings me joy, and I would urge you to find something that speaks to your heart as well.

At the different phases of the moon, find a quiet and peaceful spot outside (being mindful of your own personal safety, of course). Allow the moon to fill your mind and heart, and then start writing without worrying too much about grammar or censorship. This journal is for you and your heart, with the focus being on what it is you want to create in your life now. And by "create" I don't only mean artistic or similar endeavors. You might want to write a book or make a patchwork quilt, of course, but you might equally want a new creative approach to a difficult relationship, personal health problem, or ongoing financial issue. First write down at least five new things or issues you want to approach in a new and creative way, and then add some ideas on how you are going to go about achieving them. If you find it difficult to think of this, let it go and come back to your journal a few nights later. You might be amazed at how a little time and moon magic will come together to bring you the answers you seek.

Make a date with your journal and the moon at least once a week to check in as to how you are doing and feeling and how things are progressing with your creative

hopes and dreams. Sometimes you will change your focus and ideas as the season progresses, and that's fine too. This is not a rule book. You are free to let things go when you need to or if you no longer feel you wish to pursue a particular course.

At the end of spring, write on small pieces of paper what creative changes or goals you have achieved in this time. Bless them, then bury them under the roots of a tree or throw them onto a body of moving water under the light of the full moon. Don't forget to also bless the moon for the insights and growth she has helped you find.

The Wabi-Sabi Bird

I have a small yellow bird who is a daily visitor to the bird feeders on my deck, coming both morning and night (and tapping on the window in some indignation when I have not put out his food quickly enough). To be honest, he is not a particularly attractive bird—he has a misshapen wing, a crooked foot, and some feathers that are definitely the worse for wear. Yet he is truly beautiful in and of himself, and I derive great pleasure from watching him and seeing the bright intelligence in his little onyx eyes as he hops up and down on his wonky legs.

A while ago a friend gave me a wonderful little book called *Wabi Sabi: Japanese Wisdom for a Perfectly Imperfect*

23

Life by Beth Kempton. The book shares, in a simple and refreshing way, the traditional Japanese wisdom of wabi sabi, which basically means finding the beauty in imperfection (both our own and that of the world around us) while at the same accepting and rejoicing in the transient nature of things.

In spring, as we prepare to move into a new year with all it has to offer, we can sometimes feel overwhelmed by our lives as they are, and also what we see as our lack in various areas, be it financial, physical, or emotional. But wabi sabi, which is a way of life that is closely related and in tune with the changing seasons, reminds us that all is well and as it should be, and that includes our unique selves. We can find magic every day in the small things and gentle rituals of life. We can choose to focus on the simple and beautiful. Above all, we can find the magic in ourselves at any moment and truly accept ourselves as and who we are. That is a lesson I learn again every day from my bright little wabi-sabi bird.

Let the spring season remind us of the fact that we are human beings, not human doings! To be happy, energized, calm, and at peace is our birthright, the true gift of Mother Earth, and this joy is magic we can find anytime simply by being open to it. Life becomes good and real when we remember our true nature, the nature that is at

24

one with the trees, birds, flowers, herbs, and beautiful gifts of our world. Learning to respect and understand nature's rhythms helps us understand ourselves and those around us so much more and accept that we are all perfect, just as we have been created.

CREATE

reating one's own simple, fragrant bath and beauty remedies—and natural products for the home—is one of the most delightful and accessible ways of using green magic on an everyday basis. In spring we want to feel new, refreshed, and full of vitality; these easy recipes are quick and rewarding to make, and they will definitely grow on you and add a fresh glow to body and soul.

Skin Renewal Facial Steam

After the winter months, skin is often dry, sallow, and lacking in radiance. A simple facial steam done once or twice a week clarifies and brightens skin while removing grime and impurities. I have been using this recipe for a facial steam for many years now, and I always find it both rejuvenating and relaxing.

A word of warning: don't use facial steams on broken or irritated skin or if you have asthma or other serious breathing issues.

Half fill a large glass bowl with very hot water. Add 2 drops lemon and 3 drops each jasmine and lavender essential oils. Cleanse your face (and tie back your hair if necessary), then drape a large towel over your face and neck while holding your face above the hot water. About 8 inches away is ideal; if your face starts to feel too hot or uncomfortable, move a little farther away or stop the steam process. Remain like this for about 10–15 minutes, until the water starts to cool down, then rinse your skin with lukewarm water and pat it dry. Apply a light moisturizer. (I recommend doing a steam before bedtime, as it gives the skin a chance to relax.)

An alternative recipe, made in the same way, is the flower garden steam made using essential oils of chamomile, lavender, and rose. Use 2–4 drops of each oil or 5–6 if using only one oil.

Calm and Cleanse Body Scrub

This is only for the body, not the face, and should not be used more than once or twice a week. It is an effective and simple skin exfoliator with a beautiful scent, and it also offers the antioxidant qualities of green tea.

In a large glass jar with a secure lid, combine 1 cup Epsom salts and ½ cup each sea salt and pink Himalayan salt together with the contents of two green tea bags. Add

2 tablespoons apricot kernel or sweet almond oil, 5 drops ylang-ylang oil, and a few drops of real vanilla essence. Mix well. Stir before using, then scoop out a few tablespoons of the mix into your palm and rub gently into your torso, arms, and legs, using small circular movements (taking care around the breast area). Rinse off thoroughly and moisturize skin after use.

This scrub, stored in an airtight jar and kept in a cool place, makes enough for 5–6 applications and will last for several weeks.

Restore and Revive Facial Oil

Those of us who are no longer exactly spring chickens (myself included) often wish we could have skin that looks rejuvenated, soft, and toned. Here is a simple example of green enchantment that works wonders on all skin types.

In a small dark glass bottle, place 2 tablespoons jojoba or apricot kernel oil. (This is the base oil—you can also use rosehip oil.) Add 8 drops rose and 4 drops each lavender, frankincense, and neroli (optional) essential oils; shake vigorously and store in a cool, dark place for at least 24 hours to allow the oils to blend together. Always shake before use, and store out of direct sunlight.

To use, first cleanse your face with, ideally, a rosewater and glycerin toner (or rosewater and witch hazel if your

skin is oily), then pour a few drops of facial oil onto your hands and massage gently onto the face and throat (avoiding the eye area) using circular upward motions until the oil is well absorbed into the skin. This is a good treatment to use at bedtime so the oil continues to do its work overnight.

Spring Morning Toner

Healing and refreshing for all skin types, it will make you feel as bright as a spring morning. Marigolds are such joyful flowers, like patches of sunshine in a garden. Also known as calendula, marigolds have been used for centuries for their healing and uplifting properties.

First you will need an infusion of marigold petals. Simply place 2 cups fresh petals in a glass or china bowl and cover with boiling spring water. Leave to stand until cool, then strain off the water and restore the petals to the earth; I usually scatter them around the base of a tree.

Bring 1 cup of the marigold infusion to boil, then add 2 tablespoons dried lavender blossoms. Stir, turn off the heat, and leave for 20 minutes.

In another bowl, mix together 1 tablespoon raw honey and 3 drops of either lavender, geranium, or chamomile essential oil, then stir in ¼ cup apple cider vinegar and mix well. Add the infused marigold liquid and pour into a glass

bottle. Using cotton balls, apply to skin daily. The toner will keep for several weeks if refrigerated.

Shiny Happy Hair Spray

No, not the kind of hair spray that we used to create those tortuous hairstyles of the 1950s and '60s! This is an all-natural spray to use after shampooing—it makes hair smooth, shiny, tangle free, and smelling great to boot. It's also suitable to use on children's hair, especially when it is tangled and full of knots, and it will make the whole hair washing experience a lot more pleasant for everyone. This spray is not suitable for very oily hair, though.

In a plastic spray bottle, combine 1 cup spring or distilled water with 1 tablespoon fresh lemon juice and 2 tablespoons apple cider vinegar. Add 2 drops each clary sage, rosemary, and lemon essential oils, and shake well. Spray lightly over hair after washing, then comb through well and allow to dry naturally.

Uplifting Room Spray

We all love our home to smell fresh and inviting, and if those scents also uplift us in mood and thought, so much the better. In the spring we need both clarity and creativeness as we move into the new season and year, and this simple room spray will immediately provide both.

30

In a spray bottle, combine 1 cup spring water with ¼ cup apple cider vinegar; add 3 drops rosemary and 2 drops each mint and lemongrass essential oils. Shake well before use and spray around the walls and windows of your rooms as necessary.

Magic Home Cleaner

This is a wonderful recipe I gleaned from Jane Griffiths, a South African herbalist and gardener who has written several delightful books. There are no nasty chemicals, it smells beautiful, and it can be used anywhere in the home.

In a large spray bottle, combine 2 cups distilled water, 2 teaspoons white vinegar, 1 tablespoon baking soda, and ½ teaspoon borax (optional). Stir in 4 drops each of rosemary, lavender, and tea tree essential oils. (You can substitute eucalyptus oil for the tea tree.) Spray lightly over surfaces and wait a few minutes before wiping with a clean cloth.

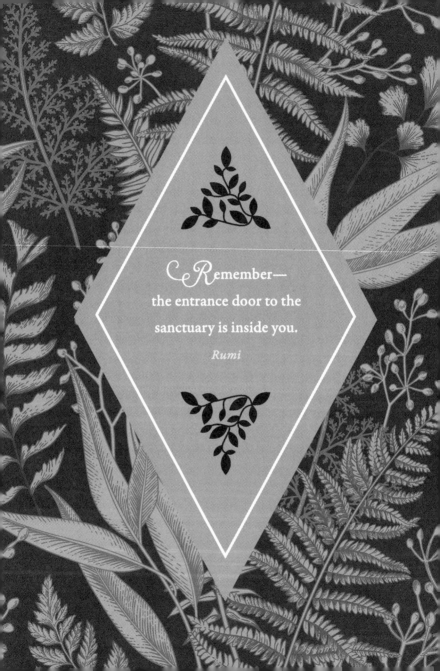

Remember—
the entrance door to the
sanctuary is inside you.

Rumi

NURTURE

urture is probably one of the most essential things in today's world, whether we are practicing self-care or nurturing those close to us or the world at large. When we take simple, natural steps to create peace, health, and serenity, it can be like a small pebble dropped in a quiet pool of water. Initially the ripples may seem small and insignificant, but as they eddy out, slowly and surely, they become a magic offering to harmony and the greater good.

In the months of spring, our area of nurture has two facets: firstly, the restoration and maintenance of physical health, which has often become depleted after the long, cold winter months and the illnesses like colds and flu that come along with frosty weather, and secondly, the need for mental focus, clarity, and creativity as we embrace the new choices, directions, and challenges that the growing season brings.

It's important to remember (and I think it's something we easily forget in our busy, crowded lives) that we cannot give to others what we don't first give to ourselves, which makes self-nurture the first and most important step on this journey.

Spring Morning Tea

Here's a lovely and simple ritual to greet spring mornings. Simply combine ¼ cup each dried lavender flowers, chamomile tea, dried lemon balm leaves, and dried peppermint in a small glass jar. Place 1–2 teaspoons in a cup, add 1 cup of freshly boiled water, and infuse for 5–10 minutes. Strain and sweeten with a little honey before drinking.

This tea not only tastes beautiful, but it also has relaxing and clarifying properties and aids with calm and focused thinking. I generally use tea bags for convenience when I don't have flowers/leaves on hand, but it's obviously just as good to use fresh or dried chamomile, too.

The Fragrant Chakras: A Simple Primer for Spring

This centuries-old belief system has much to offer us in terms of understanding and healing our bodies, thoughts, and emotions. The seven chakras each relate to a particular area of the body and also to emotional issues or problems

that may be related to that area. For this reason, I use the essential oils connected with each chakra in various ways: singly or combined, they can be added to a warm bath (just a few drops), used in massage oils, scented candles, oil burners and diffusers, or added to scented lotions and balms. Obviously the usual precautions when using essential oils must be followed, and although there are quite a number of oils generally associated with each chakra, I have selected just a few of the more widely available ones.

Starting from the base of the spine:

RED (root chakra): strength, grounding, and creating abundance. OILS: thyme, frankincense, patchouli, ylang-ylang.

ORANGE (sacral chakra): peace, joy, sexuality, and a zest for life. OILS: jasmine, rose, sandalwood, clary sage.

YELLOW (solar plexus chakra): balance, clear focus, and creating healthy personal boundaries. OILS: juniper, marjoram, lemon, sandalwood.

GREEN (heart chakra): ability to truly give and receive love; finding the heart's desire. OILS: geranium, rose, lavender, jasmine.

35

SPRING

BLUE (throat chakra): freedom, self-expression, and speaking one's truth with clarity. OILS: chamomile, basil, peppermint, rosemary.

PURPLE (third eye chakra): linked to intuition, insight, and the achieving of true dreams and higher purpose. OILS: rosemary, juniper, thyme, lemon.

WHITE or INDIGO (crown chakra): connecting to all that is spiritual and sacred in life; finding inner bliss and serenity. OILS: neroli, jasmine, rose, frankincense.

The Misery of Sinus Congestion

If you are anything like me, you may find that sinus congestion and pain linger on after the winter has passed. It's certainly not pleasant to have that throbbing, painful feeling in one's face, but fortunately there are natural remedies to ease this. The simplest is a steam inhalation of lavender and pine, which reduces both soft tissue inflammation and infection, thus reducing pain and congestion.

You will need to fill a large bowl with at least 1 pint of boiling water. Add 10 drops lavender, 5 drops pine, and 3 drops eucalyptus essential oil (optional). Hold your head, covered with a large towel, over the basin for 10–15 min-

utes. This can be repeated daily if need be, but don't use steam inhalations if you have breathing difficulties or serious asthma.

Fragrance Balm for Creating Calm and Focus

This is such a beautiful and helpful balm to use in the spring, when many of us start to feel overwhelmed by the upcoming year and its potential and prospects (whether good or not). I know I often feel quite scattered in spring as I try to plan ahead for what I want to achieve in this growing season and beyond. This simple-to-make fragrance balm can be carried with you in a small jar or pot and simply applied whenever needed to the wrists, throat, or temples. Fragrance balms make a beautiful and natural alternative to perfumes, and I find myself using them more and more, rather than commercial fragrances. Of course, you might find, after reading and using this book, that you develop your own personal preferences for essential oil blends (see the winter chapter)—in which case, feel free to have at it!

In a glass bowl set over a gently simmering pot of water, melt together 2 teaspoons beeswax beads and ¼ cup each coconut oil and sweet almond or jojoba oil. Add 5 drops each lemon, rosemary, and frankincense essential oils, then

37

SPRING

remove from the heat. The mixture will start to thicken, so pour it into small dark glass jars and leave to set completely in a cool place. Depending on your climate, you may need to add more or less beeswax to obtain a smooth but spreadable balm; if the temperatures where you live are generally quite high, I suggest keeping this balm in the refrigerator so that it doesn't melt or become oily.

Dandelion Wine
for Springtime Celebrations

Dandelion grows everywhere in the world, and often in the most inhospitable places. She is the ultimate survivor who just puts up her pretty golden head and keeps growing. Maybe there's a lesson for all of us about hanging in there until things work out for our ultimate good. This ancient plant has been used over the centuries for healing, rejuvenation, and attracting magic into our lives.

Dandelion wine was traditionally drunk at spring and summer celebrations, and it can, of course, be brewed in the traditional way, but since I lack the time, patience, and know-how for that, I start by making a strong infusion of the petals: place several cups of petals in a bowl and pour over enough boiling water to cover. Steep for at least 45 minutes, then drain the liquid very well. Allow to cool,

and store in a glass bottle or jar. Add ½ cup (or more) of this infusion to a bottle of white wine—preferably a full-bodied, fairly sweet one. Stir well and serve chilled, possibly with sparkling spring water for an intoxicating springtime punch! Drink at the height of a spring moon, and toast your resilience and growth in spite of many obstacles, just like golden dandelion.

Tulsi Tea

Tulsi is also known as holy basil, and it comes by its name with pride as it is one of the oldest known herbs, with health-giving and spiritual properties that are almost too numerous to mention. It's considered sacred to many religions and beliefs, including Hinduism and Ayurveda, but it is tulsi's noted antidepressant properties and ability to help with clear and coherent thinking that has drawn so many to this gently fragrant herb over the centuries.

Tulsi tea is easy to make and can be enjoyed at any time of the day, although I find its gentle support a good beginning to early mornings. Simply pour boiling water onto a handful of fresh leaves in a mug, steep, and strain. Add a little honey if you prefer a sweeter taste. Alternatively, you can make a flower essence (in this case, using the leaves): see the instructions for making your own flower and moon

essences in appendix C. A few drops added to a glass of spring water or dropped into a warm bathtub will bring about a definite improvement in mood and stress levels.

Lemon Verbena Massage Oil

Lemon verbena is also known by the delightful traditional names of the Herb of Grace or the Enchanter's Herb, and it is well named, for it is associated with inspiration, abundance, creativity, and healing on every level. Just the fragrance of the leaves of this tree alone are enough to inspire a positive and peaceful mindset.

To make a simple massage oil, place several handfuls of the fresh leaves in a large glass jar and cover with grapeseed, almond, or light olive oil for several weeks, until the oil has absorbed the fragrance of the leaves. Strain out the plant material and store the oil in a dark glass jar in a cool and dry place. It can be used for a healing massage or, alternatively, a little oil can be used in a diffuser or dropped in the bathtub.

Healing Spring Tub

I love bath time; showers have their place at certain times, particularly when one is in a hurry, but for true relaxation and peace, you can't beat time spent soaking quietly in the tub—preferably by candlelight, with some flowers and

40

crystals in the bathroom and perhaps some gentle music, and definitely no phones! I know this can seem like an impossible goal, especially if you have young children at home, but try to carve out private tub time for yourself at least once or twice a week.

This tub recipe is aimed at our spring goals of creativity, calm, and moving forward, and it also works wonderfully well on tired, aching, cramping muscles. The mixture can also be added to a footbath or to a small bowl when your hands are painful and aching.

Mix together 2 cups Epsom salts, 1 cup baking soda, and ½ cup pure sea salt. Stir in 5 drops each of the essential oils of your choice—for this healing spring ritual, I chose frankincense, neroli, and rosemary. Store the salts in a glass jar with a tight-fitting lid; add ½ cup to warm bathwater along with 1 cup apple cider vinegar for its cleansing and pain-relieving properties.

Casting Bottles

The name "casting bottles" comes from Tudor times and refers to small bottles containing perfumes or scented waters that were carried around and sprinkled wherever and whenever needed. (Given the lack of sanitation and general personal hygiene, I imagine they were quite a necessity!) I love making them as small gifts, tying up the

bottles with beautiful colored cords and ribbons and adding crystals, beads, feathers, or shells. This idea comes from an herbal book I used to have that was published in the 1980s; sadly, I don't remember its name or author, but I do remember she mentioned that this idea dated back several centuries.

They can also be sprinkled around a room for their cleansing and protective properties, as well as applied safely to the skin.

Place ½ pint rose hydrosol (rose water) in a clean jar and add 10 drops lavender essential oil, 1 tablespoon dried rosemary, 1 teaspoon crushed dried cloves, and a cinnamon stick broken into smaller pieces. Seal and store in a dry, sunny place for 2–3 weeks, then strain the liquid and divide between smaller bottles.

To end this section about the growing magic of spring, a quote to remember:

May you experience each
day as a sacred gift woven
around the heart of wonder.

John O'Donohue

Simple Ways to Nurture Yourself in the Spring

Self-care and nurture are not selfish, although in many ways (and especially for us women) we are conditioned to think that we should always take care of others first, and somehow caring for ourselves ends up at the very bottom of the list! However, in this year of enchanted green living, I would like us all to remember that in order to heal and grow into our best selves—the selves that are truly magical in the real sense of the word—we need to take time to understand and care for ourselves, first and foremost, without guilt.

- ◆ Think about what spring really means to you, and then go outside and experience it, even if it's chilly, raining, and windy. Notice the tiny pale leaves and bright blossoms, hear the excited calls of the birds as they prepare for a new year of babies and nests, look at the fresh blue of a spring sky.

- Let go of guilt. We all have it, and it can be crippling and hold us back from a truly joyful life. Remember no matter what we have done, we can be free of it. Write it out, talk to a friend, or simply sit quietly and ground yourself, then picture yourself as light and free, bathed in fresh white light. Burning a beautiful white candle can help with this, as can smudging (see page 189 for more information about how to do this).

- Create seasonal rituals or celebrations that are meaningful to you and your loved ones; they can be as simple or elaborate as you like. Because I live near the ocean, I always make time for special beach walks as soon as the weather starts to warm up, enjoying the fresh wind on my face. I also host a special spring tea party for a few good friends, which we enjoy in the garden with tiny cakes and cookies garnished with edible little spring blossoms.

- Find a favorite herbal tea blend (or make your own) and create a quiet morning ritual with drinking a cup of it, combined with a little personal time to read, reflect, or write in a journal.

- As mentioned in the first part of this section, spring is the perfect time for cleaning up, both inwardly and outwardly. If that seems a little daunting, commit to just clearing up one room or area of your home—quietly sorting out what you actually need and use from what you have but just don't need or use anymore. (You might be surprised at how much that amounts to.) Simplicity is enormously powerful in its ability to create both peace and change, definitely something good to focus on in the spring season.

- Honor Valentine's Day (yes, I know it's actually at the end of winter) not as the over-hyped commercial celebration it has become, but rather as a way of acknowledging the love you have in your life and the love you still have to give...and eat some chocolate, too!

- Allow yourself time to dream in this season of new beginnings and growth, remembering you are as limitless as the earth and as full of possibility.

- If you don't already have a garden of some kind, plant something in this growing season. Love and nurture it as you would yourself or anyone special, and watch it bloom before your eyes. It doesn't matter if it's just a skinny little herb or geranium seedling in a pot; it's part of nature and life.

- Depending on where you live, spring can still sometimes be quite challenging as regards weather and temperature, but now is the time to lighten up on every level. Eat lighter meals, wear lighter clothes; even if it's still cold, choose something bright and colorful instead of the darker winter hues. Light pretty candles and gather some branches of blossoms or buds to bring indoors. Remind yourself spring is finally here and the true magic of it is something you hold in your heart.

GROW

*N*o matter how small the place where you live, and even if you don't think you have any green fingers at all, it's possible to add the magic of herbs and other aromatic plants to your living and being space. The benefits are innumerable.

Some Herbs to Know

Chives (Allium schoenoprasum)

A hardy perennial that brings us its fresh green shoots in early spring, chives have a delicate onion flavor and are endlessly useful in the kitchen, added to soups, sauces, salad dressings, and baked goods and used as an aromatic garnish. The pretty fluffy purple flowers are also edible and look lovely sprinkled on salads and cold dishes.

Generally easy to grow in gardens and fairly hardy in cold climates, chives also do well in window boxes, as they enjoy lots of sun, but they also need plenty of moisture.

Keep them well trimmed and divide them into smaller plants if they seem to be overcrowded. To harvest chives, simply snip a few of the soft blades near the base of the plant. Don't cut off at the tops as if they were getting a haircut; that weakens the whole plant.

Although chives are mainly seen as a culinary herb, they also do contain sulfur compounds and various minerals (in common with other members of the onion family); as such, a chive infusion can help with colds and flu and ease indigestion.

Chives are little herbal warriors, keeping bugs and other nasties away from vegetables and other plants, so they are well worth adding to the garden. They also grow well in containers, although they will need to be split and divided every second year or so.

Lavender (Lavandula angustifolia)

This beautiful and fragrant herb needs no introduction and could have an entire book written about its history and many properties; in fact, many books have been written about this ancient herb, which is a native of the Mediterranean and is used for decorative, culinary, medicinal, and spiritual purposes. There are many varieties of lavender, but English lavender is still the best known; however,

49

all the varieties share the same powerful floral oil, lavandin. Both the flowers and leaves are used for medicinal and culinary applications since they contain the same potent oil.

Lavender grows well both in the garden and in containers as long as it has plenty of sun. It can be grown from seed or purchased as seedlings; plant in well-drained soil and don't allow it to get wet feet. Prune this hardy perennial in spring and keep cutting the flowers regularly so it will continue to produce more.

The benefits of lavender are almost too many to name, and it is justifiably considered to be the most useful and popular of all the essential oils. It is wonderful for treating burns, skin infections, and inflammations. On an emotional level, it is a powerful antidepressant and calming herb, soothing anxiety and fear and helping us to relax and sleep well. I could never be without my lavender oil and flower essence; I regard them as an essential part of a peaceful and healthy life. The dried flowers and leaves also make a wonderful addition to potpourri and fragrant sachets or dream pillows, to aid peaceful slumber.

Although lavender was not widely regarded as a culinary herb when I was growing up, that has changed a lot in recent years. However, it must be noted that a little lavender goes a long way since it is such a powerful herb and the flavor can dominate if one isn't careful. Dried flowers

and leaves can be used to make tea or added to a cup of your favorite brew. Lavender can be added to baked goods and desserts, either in the recipe or a little sprinkled on as a garnish. Try making a creamy custard with a little lavender infused in the milk for a unique taste, or make your own lavender sugar by placing a handful of dried leaves or flowers in a large glass jar and filling the jar with superfine sugar. Allow to stand in a cool, dark place for a couple of weeks, shaking the jar well every day, then strain out the lavender and you will have subtly scented lavender sugar to use in cakes and cookies.

Mint (Mentha species)

Apart from the peppermint that we are all familiar with, there are hundreds of varieties of this popular herb, including spearmint, apple mint, pineapple mint, and chocolate mint. It's a hardy little plant that does well in sunny positions with plenty of water. However, because it's also a highly invasive herb with creeping roots that tend to take over the flower bed, it's best to plant it in containers, where it will grow happily until it needs to be divided and repotted every couple of years.

We all know the fresh, clean smell of mint, but what we may not know is that it has been highly valued since biblical times and was brought to Europe after the Crusades.

51

Its volatile oil can be used to treat digestive issues like nausea, heartburn, and intestinal gas and cramping; it's also an excellent decongestant and rub for painful joints and muscles. The essential oil is a lovely addition to aromatherapy and beauty products, and it is often added to perfumes.

As we all know, mint is great in the kitchen, too; however, its bright, fresh flavor is lost in long cooking, so it is best added freshly chopped to meat dishes, sauces of all kinds, and salads. The cooling taste goes well with hot curries as well as cheese, cocktails, and fruit-based drinks. And who can resist the classic combination of mint and chocolate? Dried mint is useful in the winter months and brings a fresh taste of summer days to the table; tea can be made from mint leaves, both dried and fresh, and is wonderful as a digestive drink after a heavy or rich meal.

Mint is an excellent natural insect repellent, especially for cockroaches, ants, and mosquitoes. A little of the essential oil mixed with some spring water and sprayed or wiped onto surfaces should serve to keep the nasty critters away. Alternatively, a few drops of the oil can be added to an oil burner, especially if you are outdoors and being plagued by mosquitoes.

Garlic (Allium sativum)

Opinion is divided as to whether this pungent member of the onion family is also classed as an herb, but in my humble opinion, it is so essential in any herbal kitchen or apothecary that no one should be without it. It's a highly potent herb (both in taste and medicinal qualities) and is renowned for its antiviral, antifungal, and circulation-boosting qualities. It's been used as a remedy for respiratory problems for centuries and is believed to not only improve cardiovascular function but also lower cholesterol levels. In many Mediterranean countries, it is credited with increasing life expectancy; my Italian father ate copious quantities of garlic every day and lived to be ninety!

Although it's possible to grow your own garlic, I tend to take the easy way out and buy beautiful fresh bulbs of it at my local farmer's market. It can be used in so many creative ways, either raw or cooked. Raw garlic has a strong pungency that may be a little overpowering for some palates or too harsh for those with digestive issues. In these cases it is better cooked, when it develops a milder sweetness. A garlic bulb can be lightly rubbed with olive oil and roasted in the oven until it is soft; then the cooked garlic can be squeezed out and spread on toasted bread, vegetables, or grilled meat and chicken, which is absolutely delicious.

53

If you like raw garlic, it can be crushed and added to salad dressings, dips, marinades, sauces, and so on. When cooking with garlic, adding it towards the end of the cooking process will better preserve its unique flavor. Garlic oil is particularly useful in the kitchen and can be made in the same way as herb-infused oils (see appendix C); I also like adding herbs to the garlic, such as rosemary or basil, or a couple of little green or red chilies. And there is nothing nicer than a few crushed cloves of garlic added to some fresh butter before spreading it on hot bread, baked potatoes, or steak.

On the health front, garlic oil can be used to massage sore, painful joints and treat fungal infections of the nails or skin. (You might smell a little pungent for a while, and for sure no one will be kissing you, but the ultimate results are worth it.) Garlic is also often added to herbal tonics and tinctures and to treatments for sore throats and chest infections.

One final thought—throughout the centuries garlic has also been known for its protective qualities on the spirit plane. A friend of mine always plants lots of garlic near the front door of her home; she tells me it keeps the "varmints" away, both of the insect and human kind.

Planting by the Moon

The moon is an integral part of any spiritual or practical garden work, for she has a sacred energy that influences so much of our lives here on earth, from the tides of the oceans to our own innate human rhythms. The same applies to plants, and for centuries it was considered highly important to sow, plant, and harvest according to the different phases of the moon for the best results. This is something that still holds true today and is a way of tapping into the magic of our universe on a larger scale.

NEW TO WAXING MOON: planting herbs and leafy annuals; dreaming and preparing intentions.

WAXING TO FULL MOON: planting fruits, flowering annuals, and vines; we can focus and place our attention on desired outcomes and new beginnings in our lives.

FULL TO WANING MOON: planting bulbs, perennials, and root vegetables such as onions, carrots, and potatoes; a magic time for creation productivity and seeing the results of our efforts.

WANING TO DARK MOON: a time to harvest, remove old or dead growth and weeds; taking stock of where we are now and clearing away past blocks and obstacles.

Simple moon ceremonies, especially at times of full and new moons, are a beautiful way to acknowledge the presence and power of the moon in our lives and to thank her for her many gifts to us. They can be done singly or in groups, with those present sitting quietly under the moon, sharing simple intentions for their lives and expressing gratitude for all we have and are. The fullest phase of the moon is particularly powerful for making major life changes and addressing challenges, so we should always make space and time for being in the presence of this beautiful lunar teacher.

Herbal Astrology

Herbal magic is also linked with astrological signs, with each of the twelve signs having its own particular affiliation to certain herbs and spices.

EARTH SIGNS (Virgo, Capricorn, Taurus): mint, thyme, bergamot, patchouli, rose

AIR SIGNS (Gemini, Libra, Aquarius): lavender, marjoram, spearmint, pine, dill

FIRE SIGNS (Leo, Aries, Sagittarius): orange, rosemary, cedarwood, nutmeg, juniper

WATER SIGNS (Cancer, Scorpio, Pisces): jasmine, lemon, sandalwood, basil, ginger

56

You could consider making an astrological herb garden with different sections devoted to the twelve star signs or creating an individual small garden for yourself or as a gift for a friend. Another magical idea is making small herbal sachets or dream pillows using herbs and spices linked to a particular astrological sign.

An Enchanted Garden

A truly enchanted garden starts with your intention. Walk around your garden (or patio or balcony) and gaze upon your plants with love—even the ones that are generally regarded as weeds! To create a garden where magic grows starts with the heart, no matter how large or small your available space may be. And your garden should be a true reflection of who you are: obviously there are some "rules" as to what to plant when and where for the best results, but other than that, throw the rule book out of the window and just do what feels right for you. Experiment with the plants you instinctively feel drawn to and ultimately you will end up with a space that best works for you on every level of being.

For your garden to truly be a sanctuary, a place where you can refresh yourself and others on every level, you can add a few very special features to make it even more enchanted. Water is life. If you can add a small water

feature to the garden, it becomes truly magical. It doesn't have to be fancy; even a small birdbath will add a touch of enchantment to the space.

Stones are symbols of earth energy. Try collecting stones that speak to you on some level, and arrange them in a corner of your garden or collect them in a small basket or dish as part of your indoor garden. Crystals, too, are a potent force for positive change, love, and healing. Particularly suitable ones in a garden would be amethyst, rose quartz, jasper, malachite, and turquoise.

Since an enchanted garden is a place you will want to spend a lot of time in, ensure there is a space to sit, a place for quiet reflection and meditation, either alone or with others. If you will be spending time in the garden at night, a few simple lanterns or candles are beautiful (obviously, ensure fire safety at all times). It's probably best to simply carry a few candles with you or place a few tealights in sturdy containers on the ground.

TASTE

*I*t's somewhat an overused cliché that the kitchen is the heart of the home, but like many such sayings it contains absolute truth and wisdom. No matter the size or style of your home, the kitchen is almost certainly where the true magic happens, the nurturing of body and soul on a daily basis. And if it isn't, and you don't like cooking or see it as a painful but necessary chore, I hope that some of these simple yet delicious recipes will help you change your mind.

Green magic is, after all, at its most accessible to us in the kitchen. Everything we cook with has its roots in Mother Earth—fruits, vegetables, dairy products, eggs, chickens, herbs, spices, and fish (after all, the oceans cover most of the surface of this place we call home). And particularly where herbs and other plants are concerned, using them creatively in the food we make is the best way of getting the health and taste benefits they offer.

In spring the focus in the kitchen turns away from the heavier and more sustaining foods of winter, like thick soups and casseroles, to a menu that celebrates the simultaneous brightening of the days and our souls. We need to eat fresher, lighter foods that will support us nutritionally as we start the journey through the year. A visit to your local farmer's market will surely give you lots of inspiration with the natural bounty it offers.

Salsa Verde
(with a Difference!)

MAKES ABOUT 1 CUP SAUCE

The famous "green sauce" of Italy is usually made with basil and flat-leafed parsley, as well as capers and anchovies, but I have given it a revamp with cilantro and mint to make a sauce that sings with bright Eastern flavors. It's beautiful served with grilled fish or chicken, or spooned over rice or steamed vegetables; add a dollop to salad dressing or stir into curries and stir-fry dishes. The leaves and stems of fresh cilantro have a cooling, detoxifying, and grounding effect, and cilantro has been used for centuries as a digestive aid. Of course you can use any herbs you prefer, and you can add 2 tablespoons of traditional capers if you like them.

- **1½ cups fresh cilantro leaves and stems**
- **2 tablespoons fresh lemon juice**
- **½ cup fresh mint leaves**
- **1 chopped green chilli (optional)**
- **2 garlic cloves, peeled and chopped**
- **4 salted anchovies (optional)**
- **2 tablespoons olive oil**
- **½ teaspoon salt**

Combine all the ingredients in a blender or food processor, and blend until finely chopped but not a homogeneous paste; the sauce should still have some texture. Add a little more oil or lemon juice to the mixture if it is very dry, then spoon into a glass jar and store in the fridge. It will keep for 7–10 days refrigerated.

Little Chive Pancakes

MAKES ABOUT 16 PANCAKES

Delicate chives with their subtle onion flavor look like spring on a plate; here they are added to little yeast pancakes, which are akin to Russian blini (minus the buckwheat). They taste great with smoked salmon and some thinly sliced red onion. Or try topping them with cream cheese flavored with garlic and black pepper, Parma ham and pesto, or a dollop of creamy scrambled egg and crisp bacon slivers. I love serving them for a special breakfast or

61

tea party treat. Always make them small—they just work better that way.

> **1 teaspoon sugar**
> **1 teaspoon active dried yeast**
> **1 cup milk, lukewarm**
> **1 tablespoon plus 1 cup plain flour**
> **½ teaspoon salt**
> **1 egg**
> **2 tablespoons melted butter**
> **¼ cup finely snipped chives**
> **Butter or oil for frying**

Mix the sugar and yeast together in a bowl, then add the milk. Sprinkle 1 tablespoon of flour over the top, cover the bowl, and leave to stand for 20 minutes, until the mixture is bubbly. Combine the cup of flour and salt with the yeast batter, egg, and melted butter. Beat until smooth and thick. Fold in the chopped chives. Cover the bowl and leave to stand for 45 minutes, then beat again.

Heat a little butter or oil in a heavy skillet and drop tablespoonfuls of batter into the pan. Only cook 3–4 at a time, as they spread. Cook for 2 minutes, then turn with a spatula once bubbles appear on the surface; cook on the other side for 3 minutes, until golden. Keep cooked pancakes covered—the pancakes are nicest served warm and fresh.

Pepper and Potato Frittata
with Basil and Feta

SERVES 4

This is such a simple, all-purpose dish—perfect kitchen magic! It can be served hot, warm, or cold for breakfast, brunch, or on a picnic, dished up in wedges straight out of the skillet. Eggs are a powerful symbol of spring, the rebirth of the earth, and nature, making this the perfect dish for the spring season. Basil is a wonderful, aromatic herb, not just in the kitchen but also as a powerful healer and rejuvenator for body and soul. Instead of red pepper, you can use lightly steamed stalks of fresh asparagus or baby spinach leaves.

> **2 cups new or baby potatoes**
> **2 tablespoons olive oil**
> **1 red pepper, seeded and chopped**
> **1 small onion, finely chopped**
> **2 garlic cloves, finely chopped**
> **6 eggs**
> **Salt and pepper to taste**
> **2 ounces feta cheese, crumbled**
> **Handful of fresh basil leaves**

First, peel and boil the baby potatoes until just tender, then drain and cool by standing them in a bowl of cool water for 10 minutes before slicing thinly.

63

Heat olive oil in a heavy, deep skillet and sauté the pepper, onion, and garlic until soft and fragrant. Add the prepared baby potatoes to the skillet and spread out to form an even layer. Beat the eggs until thick and add salt and pepper to taste. Pour the eggs over the vegetables and continue to cook until they are set and golden brown. (You can also do this under the broiler if your skillet is ovenproof.)

Remove from the stove, cool for a few minutes, then sprinkle the crumbled feta and the torn basil leaves over the top. This frittata is nicest served at room temperature, sliced straight from the skillet, with a few fresh salad greens and some good bread on the side.

Pasta with Lemon, Anchovies, and Dill

SERVES 3–4

This is my version of a traditional Italian dish, which is full of bright and strong flavors and topped with delicate sprigs of fresh dill and crispy breadcrumbs. Dill has been used for centuries as a digestive and antispasmodic herb. Although its distinctive taste is not loved by everyone, give it a chance—you might find it really grows on you.

The anchovies are optional and can be omitted from the recipe. A nice alternative would be some good quality seedless black olives, halved—but in that case, I would replace the dill with chopped basil or oregano.

64

2 tablespoons olive oil

2 slices of white bread, crumbled

½ stick of butter

8 anchovy fillets, drained (optional)

2 garlic cloves, crushed

Juice and rind of 1 small lemon

Freshly ground black pepper

8 ounces linguine or spaghetti

1 handful fresh dill leaves

Parmesan cheese (optional)

First, make the crispy breadcrumbs—heat the olive oil in a skillet and fry the crumbled bread until golden and crispy. Drain well and set aside in a bowl.

In a small saucepan, melt together the butter and anchovy fillets, then stir in the garlic, lemon, and black pepper to taste. Mash the anchovy with a spoon, then cook until a sauce is formed.

In the meantime, boil up a large pot of salted water and cook the pasta until done to your liking. Drain well and toss with the anchovy sauce before serving in heated bowls topped with the breadcrumbs, sprigs of fresh dill, and Parmesan.

Carrot, Lemon, and Mint Salad

SERVES 4–6

I love the fresh simplicity of this healthy salad that looks and tastes like spring. It makes a colorful addition to a lunch table or the perfect side dish for curries and spicy foods. Mint is such a fresh and cleansing herb, and it aids healthy digestion; lemon balm leaves or lemon thyme also work well.

> **4–6 medium carrots**
> **1 red onion, finely sliced**
> **1 garlic clove, crushed**
> **Juice of 2 lemons**
> **½ cup olive oil**
> **½ teaspoon ground cumin**
> **½ teaspoon ground coriander**
> **Small handful of fresh mint**

Peel and grate the carrots, not too finely; place them in a glass bowl and add the onion and garlic. To make the dressing, mix together the lemon juice, olive oil, ground cumin and coriander, and the chopped mint. Toss the carrot mixture with the dressing and then chill well before serving, topped with additional mint leaves.

Chocolate Mint Pots

In pagan beliefs, spring was the season to celebrate sensuality and all the senses, and let us not forget Valentine's Day, which comes at the very tail end of winter but is still the celebration of passion and romance. This is an old recipe from my mother, but the mint is my addition since the combination of chocolate and mint is such a classic and delicious one. Although this recipe is made as six individual desserts, it can be made in one larger dish.

1 cup milk

5 ounces good quality dark chocolate, chopped

1 teaspoon vanilla extract

2 eggs, separated

2 tablespoons superfine sugar

1 cup single cream

1 tablespoon finely chopped mint leaves

Confectioner's sugar to serve

Preheat oven to 400° F. Warm milk and chocolate together in a saucepan over low heat until the chocolate has melted. Stir in the vanilla and remove from the heat. Beat the egg yolks and sugar together until thick and pale, then stir into the milk mixture. Stir in the cream. Whip the egg whites until fluffy, then fold gently into the egg and milk mixture. Lastly, add the mint leaves.

Divide the mixture between 6 individual baking cups or ramekins or one larger dish. Set these dishes in a larger baking dish and carefully pour in boiling water to come halfway up the sides of these dishes. Bake for 25–30 minutes, until the mixture has risen slightly and the surface looks crusty. Remove from the water bath and leave to cool. Refrigerate. Before serving, dust with confectioner's sugar and a few additional mint leaves.

The Herbal Pantry for Spring

When the earth comes to life in spring, we need to enjoy her gifts for as long as possible, and for me that includes making lots of herbal pestos and pastes, which are a wonderful way of eating goodly quantities of fresh herbs in a form that is both delicious and nutritious. Traditional pesto is made with both nuts (generally pine nuts or walnuts) and cheese, but I usually omit the nuts since so many people are allergic to them. The best thing about pesto is that you can use your favorite herbs, either singly or in combination: the recipe below is just a guideline. You can

68

also omit the cheese if you wish to make the pesto suitable for vegans.

Oregano and Parsley Pesto

I prefer using flat-leaved parsley for this recipe since I think it has more flavor, but if you can only get the curly variety it will still be good. Spread on bread, stir a little of the pesto into dips, sauces, or marinades, use as a topping for vegetables, and spoon onto grilled cheese sandwiches or omelets.

> 1 cup fresh parsley leaves, chopped
>
> ½ cup fresh oregano leaves, chopped
>
> 2 cloves fresh garlic, crushed
>
> ¼ cup grated Parmesan cheese
>
> 1 small green chili, chopped
>
> 1 tablespoon fresh lemon juice
>
> Approximately 2 tablespoons olive oil
>
> Salt and pepper to taste

This is best made using a mortar and pestle, but you can use a food processor if you prefer. Combine the parsley and oregano, and crush together to form a paste. Stir in the garlic, cheese, chili, and lemon juice, then gradually add enough olive oil to make a thick, smooth mixture (you may need more or less oil). Add salt and pepper to taste, then store in an airtight jar in the refrigerator for up to 2 weeks.

SUMMER

Abundance & Passion

ummer is the favorite season for so many of us. Bright, seemingly endless days and warm starry nights. Feeling free and open in light summer clothes, walking with our bare feet on fresh grass or cool beach sand. After spring's light and soft colors, now we have vibrant hues and intoxicating scents offered as a gift of abundance from Mother Earth.

Above all, we have a renewed sense of being truly alive and of the life blood that flows in and through each of us. When we talk about passion, we often only refer to it in the context of romantic relationships, but passion is infinitely more than that. It's a way to live our radiant and unique lives. When we combine our passions—whatever they may be—with commitment and effort, we can truly find power and grace.

And summer also reminds us that time passes—she won't be here forever, and neither will we; the present moment is all we have. As such, this is where true enchantment lies, not in memories of the past or hopes of the as-yet-unknown future. In this beautiful season, it's okay to be just who and what we are, precious and perfect in our individual gifts, while basking in the joy of our earth openhearted, radiant, and aware.

72

HEART NOTES

*I*n this section you will find a few simple thoughts and rituals to truly bring the warmth and enchantment of summer alive... after all, it's the perfect season to be outside and resting in the gifts of nature! Savor and celebrate these special months as you find both sanctuary and peace in the warm summer days.

Meet a Flower

Probably we all have had the experience of meeting someone who is a total stranger up to that point and yet instantly feeling a deep connection with them, as if we are on the same wavelength or sharing a similar vibe. This is entirely understandable: as human beings we possess definite energy fields and vibrations that can be picked up by others who are in tune with their own psychic energy. The natural world possesses this same energy—every animal, insect, flower, leaf, tree, and stone carries its own unique vibration to which we can also attune ourselves. When we are able to tap into these gentle, subtle messages, they can do much to restore hope, healing, and joy in our lives. This is the underlying principle of Dr. Edward Bach's work with flower remedies, as with all the others since who have done valuable work in this particular field. Bach believed, as have many others since, that certain plants, trees, and flowers possess qualities that can help us move past emotional and spiritual blocks towards a new and joyful way of being.

When we feel particularly drawn to a certain herb, flower, or other plant, I believe it is because on a subconscious level we know that plant has something to share with us—a healing to offer or a light to shine on something in our lives. For example, I have always been strongly drawn to nasturtiums, with their bright, sunny colors that are so reminiscent of summer and sunshine. I was not entirely surprised to learn that these flowers are strongly linked to helping us lose the fear of the unknown and move forward to new opportunities with confidence and clarity—to becoming truly ourselves rather than just "going with the flow," as these are issues I, like so many others, have struggled with over the years.

Obviously, we will all feel drawn to different flowers and plants, usually because something in them speaks directly to something in our heart and soul. This summer, try to

74

spend some time sitting with flowers. You can do this outside in a garden or park, or you can gather them and bring them into your home. Relax and study the flower, breathing very slowly and deeply. Allow your thoughts to focus on what this little plant is trying to offer you, the gentle lessons she or he is trying to share (yes, flowers have masculine or feminine energies, too).

If you discover a particular bloom resonates with your energy in a personal way, there are many ways to enjoy this magic. Obviously you can grow them or keep them around in your home, or you can also create your own flower and moon essences from them (see ideas for this in appendix C). Flower essences not only can be taken in water but can also be added to the bathtub or to a body or room mist. If essential oils of your favorite flower are available, they can be used in any of the ways described in this book; for example, added to baths, oils, balms, and fragrances or burned in candles or oil diffusers.

An excellent reference for much greater insight into this beautiful world is *The Magic of Flowers* by Tess Whitehurst. This wonderful and in-depth book became my go-to resource when I was studying advanced flower essences and therapies, and it remains a much-loved volume on my bookshelf.

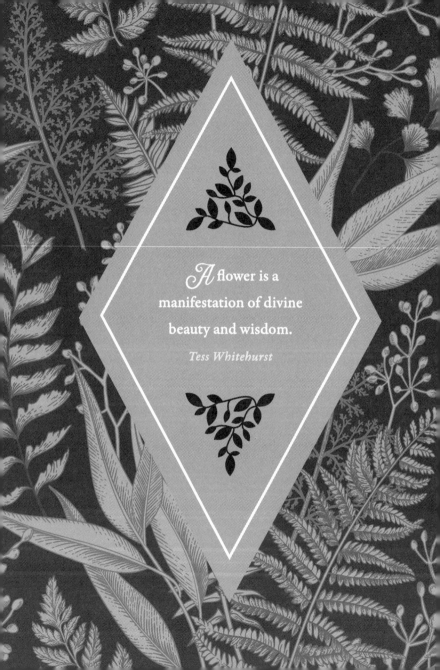

A flower is a
manifestation of divine
beauty and wisdom.

Tess Whitehurst

Walk Barefoot on the Grass

Perhaps you are like me—as soon as you are home, off go the shoes! I have always preferred being barefoot, even when I was growing up; I spent most of my time without shoes unless I was forced to wear them; it drove my mother mad. But today, so many years later, I think I reaped the benefits in that I have exceptionally healthy feet that have always served me so well and never given me any real problems.

Yet there is a far deeper meaning to us being barefoot as nature always intended us to be. Without covering on our feet, we are back on solid ground, so to speak, with a far greater awareness of our surroundings. It also gives not only our feet and ankles but also our legs, knees, and pelvis a gentle workout. Grounding reconnects us with the energy and power of the earth, whether we need to calm down and release excess energy or access greater personal strength when we are feeling tired and depleted. For this reason, it's a good idea to start or end the day by grounding yourself, preferably outside. Grounding is also helpful before meditating, doing yoga and the like, or when going into a potentially stressful situation.

In summer we should make a point of trying to walk barefoot on grass as often as we can, preferably while it

is still wet with dew. In many cultures and beliefs, this is considered an important health practice, one which helps to ease stress, anxiety, depression, and insomnia. We are grounded again, at one with the energy of the earth, which is of course our inherent energy too. Outside on a summer morning—what more natural and beautiful place to be?

Open the Heart
Rose Ritual

The rose is certainly one of the most-loved flowers, if not the most loved. The beauty of this flower, combined with her exquisite fragrance and powerful effect on the human psyche on so many levels, makes her the perfect partner when we need to restore and renew the heart, which can become constricted by rejection, trauma, and grief. Oftentimes we close up emotionally and decide it's less painful to live this way, but just like a closed hand, a closed heart cannot receive love, hope, and new grace.

This gentle and healing ritual is perfect for when you need to open yourself up again with trust and hope, and find the clarity and confidence we all need to give love, firstly to ourselves and then to others, while at the same time being able to receive it with joy and acceptance.

In the evening, find a quiet and peaceful spot, either indoors or out, and place a small posy of roses (or even

78

just a single perfect bloom in a vase) between two pink or red candles. Burn a little rose oil in a diffuser or rub a few drops on your hands. Sit quietly and fold your hands over your heart. Close your eyes and imagine your heart is like a beautiful rose: first a tight bud and then slowly, slowly opening its petals to the light and coming into its full magnificence. Extend your hands and say the following words:

> *I am loved. The love I need is there, inside*
> *me. It is safe in my heart. I am loved.*
> *I can create a life full of love and beauty*
> *for myself and others. I am love. Nothing*
> *can take that from me. And so it is.*

This ritual can be repeated whenever you need it and is also beautiful shared with a close friend or significant other.

Create a Nature Mandala

A mandala (the word means "circle" in Sanskrit) is a form of repeating patterns, generally circular, that is used to create a meditative and deepening sense of self and spirituality. Many cultures and beliefs have used mandalas for centuries, and they have become increasingly popular again in the twenty-first century as we seek calm, clarity, and spiritual awareness.

79

In the summer, I want to urge you to take walks—lots of walks, long walks in nature. There is no urgency, no rush, just being out there with our Mother Earth and her many gifts. And on these walks you will find many small offerings: leaves, pebbles, sticks, blossoms. (If you also walk on the beach, you will find shells, sea glass, and bits of seaweed too.) And if you live near a bird sanctuary, as I am fortunate enough to do, you'll find lots of colorful feathers left by these little angelic messengers.

Carry a basket with you to collect these natural offerings, then create your own green mandala in a quiet and beautiful spot, perhaps a shady corner of your garden or on the beach. There are no real rules as to making a nature mandala; it is a process of the heart, and you should simply follow your inward guidance as you start to build your mandala from the center outwards. You may find thoughts and words coming to you that serve as inspiration for your creation; I once made a mandala of herbs, starting with a ring of tiny thyme flowers and then going through successive circles to the outer ring, which was composed of lavender stalks and beautiful small white feathers. On that particular day, I felt I was growing and part of something bigger than myself, and that became my focus and meditation.

You will find your own personal meditative focus creating a mandala; this is also a particularly lovely and rewarding activity to share with children, who are usually both enthusiastic and endlessly creative when working with nature. Just one note: if possible, choose plants that are abundant or have already fallen—don't rip out all the daffodils in the flower bed, for example. And if you need something growing on someone else's property, ask permission first. I found this out the hard way, having once gotten into a great deal of trouble for taking some roses that I wrongly assumed were growing wild near my home.

CREATE

*I*n summer we can tap into our earth's bounty in so many ways and truly bring the garden into our bodies, minds, and hearts. This abundant season is also one where we want to feel fresh, renewed, and full of joy, even on the hottest days, and often we need the gift of herbs and flowers to help with that. Simple and natural creations for body and home are the best way to truly enjoy summer with all our senses.

Summer Breeze Dusting Powder

We all want to keep fresh and dry on hot and humid summer days, but of course sweating is an entirely natural process, a way in which the body not only regulates its core temperature but also removes toxins. For this reason, I really don't like using either commercial deodorants or antiperspirants, which are generally full of strange chemical ingredients. An infinitely better alternative is a gentle dusting powder, which can be applied anytime you feel hot

and bothered or your skin is itchy and irritated. This powder is also gentle enough to be used on babies or children, although in that case I would amend the recipe and just add 5 drops of neroli and chamomile oils instead.

Mix 1 cup cornstarch and ½ cup baking soda together very well, then spread the mixture out on a large baking sheet or board. Sprinkle over 10 drops each of lavender, neroli, and tea tree essential oils, and stir through the mixture well. Allow to dry for an hour before placing the mixture in an airtight jar or shaker bottle. Store for a few days before use to allow the fragrance to develop. The dusting powder does not need to be refrigerated, but keep it in a cool, dry place and use within 3–4 months.

Bugs-Away Spray

A little annoyance of the summer time: bugs, mosquitoes, and other little varmints that can become a real nuisance. But this simple spray will deter the most determined of them—and it smells lovely and is quite harmless, which cannot be said of many commercial sprays. Spray lightly on the body or clothes while avoiding the eye and nose area, please.

Combine 1 cup of witch hazel and 1 tablespoon of vegetable glycerin in an 8-ounce plastic spray bottle, then add 10 drops citronella oil and 8 drops each lemongrass and

83

geranium essential oils. (You can substitute lemon verbena oil for the lemongrass, if preferred.) Shake very well to combine. The spray does not need to be refrigerated, but it should be kept out of direct light and heat and used within 6 months.

Another entirely natural insect repellent is the herb rue, which is not grown as much as it used to be in years gone by, when it was used medicinally (not something that is generally recommended these days). It has a strange scent, almost impossible to describe, which seems to be particularly appealing to dogs—well, my dogs liked it anyway, like a form of canine catnip! If you do grow rue, simply stand a few stems and leaves in a glass of water in your kitchen, or wherever you are being plagued by flies and other insects, and you will find they will disappear very quickly.

Cucumber and Aloe Vera Gel

Where I grew up in South Africa there were several large aloe vera plants growing in the garden; when someone got a cut or graze or injury of any kind, my mom would pick a few of the fleshy leaves, snap them in half, and apply the gel inside the leaf directly to the afflicted area. It's a truly wonderful healing plant that also has protective properties, warding off evil spirits and the like. Cucumber is naturally cooling and healing too, so together they make a wonder-

ful combination, excellent for overly dry, irritated, and inflamed skin (often a side effect of the summer heat); they also work well for sore and painful joints. I have an artist friend who swears by this gel as an analgesic and cooling remedy for his arthritic fingers after hours of painting.

I add a little tea tree or mint oil because I like the fragrance, but you can leave the oil out. If you don't have your own aloe vera plants, the gel is easy to buy, but please choose the most natural one you can, without additives, if possible.

Peel and chop 1 medium cucumber, then place in a blender with 1 cup spring or distilled water and 8 drops each of peppermint and tea tree essential oils (if using). Blend very well to form a thick juice, then strain thoroughly, ensuring no bits of skin or seeds remain in the liquid. Place ½ cup aloe vera gel in a bowl, then gradually stir in the cucumber juice mixture until it is well amalgamated. (If it's a bit runny, you might need more gel.) Store the gel in a sterilized glass jar and keep in the fridge, particularly if the weather is hot and humid. Use within 2–3 weeks.

Garden Gifts Hand and Foot Scrub

Feet get dirty in the summer—and that's good; it's how they were meant to be. Hands, too, especially when you have been gardening and digging in the dirt. Rinse hands

and feet, then use a few scoops of this scrub, rubbing it in well, and rinse off thoroughly before applying a little skin moisturizing cream.

Combine 1 cup each pure (non-iodized) sea salt and Epsom salts with 2 teaspoons sweet almond oil, 10 drops rosemary essential oil, and 5 drops each lavender and sage essential oils. Mix together well and store in a glass jar with a tight-fitting lid. Store in a cool, dry place and use within 3–4 months.

Heart's Garden Body Cream

Both rose and frankincense carry powerful qualities for love, passion, healing, and regeneration; this simple cream with its intoxicating fragrance is wonderful for creating a joyful spirit, and it's a gentle reminder of how good life can be. You can substitute jasmine oil for the frankincense, if you prefer.

In a small bowl set over a pan of gently simmering water, heat together 2 tablespoons almond or jojoba oil, 1 teaspoon beeswax (grated or pellets), and 1 tablespoon cocoa butter. The mixture must not boil but just gently melt together. Then stir in 10 drops each rose and frankincense essential oils, and remove from the heat. Allow to cool, stirring often, until the mixture thickens. Pour into a small glass jar, and keep in a cool, dark place. Use within 4–6 months.

86

Vanilla-Coconut
After-Sun Soothing Balm

We are all sometimes guilty of this: we forget to apply enough SPF cream or we spend a little too much time in the sun and next thing we have a red, painful sunburn. This balm not only soothes and rehydrates skin but also smells absolutely delicious.

In a double boiler or a bowl set over a pan of hot water, melt together ½ cup pure, unrefined coconut oil, ½ cup sweet almond or jojoba oil, and 2 tablespoons cocoa butter. (Shea butter can also be used.) When the mixture has melted, remove from the heat and cool for 15 minutes. Stir in 20 drops of either vanilla or neroli essential oil (or 10 drops of each). Stir well and pour in a pretty glass jar. Use within 2–3 months. If your climate is very hot and humid, keep the balm in the fridge.

Florida Water

I first encountered Florida Water some years ago—when a dear old family friend gave me a little bottle, saying it "was like cologne, only a little magical!" At the time, although I certainly loved its delicate rose and citrus fragrance, I did not take much notice of her words. It's only relatively recently that I have discovered more about this fragrant cologne and its many uses down the years as a tool

for blessings, protection, enchantment, and accessing the world of the spirits. If you sprinkle a little on your pillow at night, apparently you will have prophetic dreams of the future, too! Florida Water, which was first mentioned as long ago as 1808, is a new-world version of the traditional eau de cologne from Europe but with the addition of lavender and cloves. It was apparently named for the legendary Fountain of Youth, located in Florida, and has been widely used in various religious and spiritual practices.

It is possible to buy Florida Water, and there are also many different recipes out there, some more elaborate than others and calling for the addition of fresh scented rose petals, which are not always easy to come by. My recipe, while simpler, still carries all the fragrance and charm of the original cologne.

In a large jar, place the juice and rind of one orange and one lemon, a handful of fresh lavender flowers, 1 teaspoon dried cloves, and ½ teaspoon dried cinnamon. Pour over ½ cup rose water, then add 6 drops each rose, lavender, neroli, and bergamot essential oils together with 3 drops tincture of benzoin, a natural preservative.

Pour over this 2 cups vodka—there must be at least enough alcohol to completely cover the mixture in the jar. Cover the jar and place it in a cool, dark place for at least

a month or longer and shake the jar well every few days. Then strain the mixture through filter paper very well, removing all loose particles, and pour into small glass bottles. The mixture can also be diluted with an equal part of spring or distilled water. Keeps well if stored in a cool place.

Refreshing Citrus Face Splash

This light and lovely facial splash will give your face a fresh glow on the warmest summer days. Although this is fine for most facial types, it's better not to use it on very dry or damaged skin. If you can't find orange flower water, rose water can be substituted.

Mix together ½ cup each witch hazel and orange flower water. Stir in 1 tablespoon vegetable glycerin and 5 drops each neroli and lemon essential oils. Store in a small bottle and apply to the face and neck with a soft cotton wool pad, avoiding the eye area.

Summer Fresh Aroma Disks

MAKES ABOUT 8–10 SMALL AROMA DISKS

No, not those awfully fake-smelling air-freshening products one can buy but something entirely natural to place in your bathroom, bedroom, kitchen—in fact, just about anywhere you would like to add a fresh herbal or floral note.

Place 2 cups baking soda in a glass bowl, then stir in approximately ¾ cup spring or distilled water and 1 teaspoon vegetable glycerin. Mix together with your hands to form a thick, smooth paste. Add up to 15 drops of your favorite essential oils; I like to use lemon, geranium, lavender, or mint. Press into little soap molds—small muffin tins also work well—and leave to dry for a couple of days, then press out of the molds. Place wherever you need—I like to keep them in shallow, small glass or china bowls. They should last about a month, after which the fragrance dissipates and they need to be replaced.

NURTURE

*T*he long, bright days of summer bring us joy, celebration, and an even greater reason to celebrate not only our beautiful earth but also the magic that lives within each one of us, body, heart, and soul. In summer we can use the warm and fragrant blessings around us to truly support our well-being in every aspect, from physical health to emotional and spiritual nurture.

Peaceful Nights Pillow Mist

On hot summer nights it can be difficult to fall asleep or to remain in a comfortable, deep sleep if one starts to be overheated or restless. This is a simple recipe that can be kept in a small spray bottle next to the bed; just spray a little onto your pillow and sheets before bedtime, and you will find peaceful and restful nights await!

Combine 1 cup distilled or spring water, ½ cup apple cider vinegar, and ¼ teaspoon borax in a plastic spray bottle. Add 5 drops each of lavender, jasmine, and sandalwood

essential oils, and shake very well to combine. Shake again before using the spray.

After-Sun Soothing Tub

If you have the misery of sore, sunburned skin, a soak in this soothing tub should help cool you down and ease discomfort. But please note that serious sunburn is potentially dangerous, especially for children; seek professional medical advice or visit the emergency room if you are concerned.

For more minor cases of sunburn, try this soothing recipe. Run a tub of lukewarm water, not hot, and stir in ½ cup each baking soda and Epsom salts. When the salts have dissolved, add 5 drops each lavender and geranium essential oils; both are excellent for burns and inflammation. Sit in the tub for at least 15–20 minutes, allowing the water to cover any sunburned areas. After climbing out the tub, pat your skin dry very gently before slipping into some light cotton pajamas; for this reason, it's best to do this just before bedtime. Apply the vanilla-coconut soothing balm on page 87 for even greater comfort.

Achy Head Balm

The heat of summer often brings with it more headaches, but this soothing balm works wonders rubbed into the

temples or back of the neck, and it is gentle enough to use on anyone.

In a glass bowl set over a pan of simmering water, combine ⅓ cup sweet almond oil with a handful of chopped bay leaves, a handful of fresh lavender flowers, 2 tablespoons mint leaves, 2 tablespoons rosemary leaves, and 1 tablespoon crushed coriander seeds. Heat very gently for 2–3 hours so the flavors can infuse; at no time should the mixture boil. Then strain the infused oil into a bowl or jug and stir in 1 tablespoon grated beeswax, which should melt in the heat of the oil. Add 6 drops each of lavender and rosemary essential oils. Stir the mixture well until it starts to thicken, then pour it into a sterilized glass jar and store in a cool, dry place until needed.

For a pick-me-up balm when your energy is flagging in the summer heat or you are traveling, follow the above recipe but use lavender, rose, and bergamot essential oils, and omit the bay leaves and rosemary.

Summer Sunrise Tea

A cheerful pick-me-up for the morning, this tea is especially helpful on days when you feel a little overwhelmed by all the tasks you have to do or are just in a low, uninspired mood.

93

In an airtight jar, combine ½ cup each jasmine and chamomile tea. Add ¼ cup each dried lemon balm and scented geranium leaves—also a handful of dried borage (starflowers), if you can find it—and mix together well.

To make tea, place 2 teaspoons of the mixture in a mug or cup and pour a cup of just boiled water over the top. Allow to steep for 10 minutes, then strain and add honey to taste. A thin slice of lemon floated in the cup makes the tea even more sunny and uplifting.

New Horizons Fragrant Oil

Beautiful though summer is, it can also sometimes seem daunting. There is the sense of fresh abundance, passion, and opportunities waiting for us, but sometimes we shrink back from these new horizons, preferring to stay in the comfort of the familiar and usual for fear of hurt, rejection, or failure. This is, of course, entirely natural and human; we don't want to relive unhappy past experiences or times of rejection that caused us to shut down and believe we weren't good enough, deserving enough, or just enough on any level. Which of course we are, and always have been; just by being here on this earth, we are a precious and unique part of the cycle of life.

Quiet meditation and reflection are helpful if we are feeling stuck or unable to truly enjoy life as it is, as is talking

94

to someone trusted and caring or seeking professional support if we feel that is needed. This simple aromatherapy oil is also very effective as a day-to-day way of helping us to engage more fully with life while being open to our own possibilities. Pour ¼ cup sweet almond or jojoba oil in a small dark glass bottle and then add 10 drops neroli and 3 drops each chamomile and geranium essential oils.

Keep the oil in a cool place. It can be used in various ways—for example, a few drops can be added to bathwater or rubbed on the hands. Use the oil in a burner or diffuser, or make a simple room mist by adding a few drops to a spray bottle of distilled water to which you have also added 2 tablespoons of apple cider vinegar. Use this magical mixture whenever you need to feel positive and joyful about yourself and your life.

Jasmine Moon Essence

Flower essences are generally made using the sun method (see appendix C), but there are also times when we want to access the unique energy and spirituality of the moon when preparing an essence. It's basically a very simple process, but you do need to wait for a full moon in a clear night sky and also have to be able to access a few handfuls of fresh jasmine blossoms.

95

Fill a large, clear glass bowl with spring water. Carry a basket to the flowers and gently snip them into the basket, touching them as little as possible. Drop the flowers onto the surface of the water in the bowl, and leave the bowl in the moonlight for at least 3–4 hours or longer if you can. Then remove the flowers with a small twig and sprinkle them around the base of a tree or into a body of running water. Take a 4-ounce glass dropper bottle and fill it half full with water from the jasmine bowl. Pour the remaining water away, again around the base of a tree. Fill the bottle to the top with brandy; you have now created the mother essence, which will last for 1–2 years if stored in a cool, dry place.

To use the jasmine essence, take 5–6 drops of the mother essence and place in a small 1-ounce glass bottle. Fill the bottle with brandy and store in a cool, dark place. Add a few drops of the essence to a glass of water or bathwater. You can also use the essence in a cup of jasmine or rose tea, or even a glass of sparkling champagne!

Jasmine can show us how to renew the sense of joy and abundance in our lives, especially when we are feeling stuck or impoverished on any level, be it practical, financial, or emotional. Using this essence helps us to worry and stress less so we may enjoy more of the many blessings in our lives every single day.

♦ It's very important to keep yourself well hydrated at all times. Fill jugs with spring water, still or sparkling, then add a few sprigs of herbs such as rosemary, thyme, or lemon balm, a couple of strawberries or thin slices of fresh orange or lemon, and plenty of ice. Sip and enjoy all through the day. Herbal teas are also both hydrating and delicious in summer, especially when served chilled and topped with fresh mint and thin slices of citrus.

♦ If possible, take some time off in the middle of the day, when the summer heat is at its peak. You don't have to sleep but you do need to lie down in a cool spot for at least twenty minutes and let your body totally relax, which is actually as beneficial as taking a nap. Even better, lie down on the grass under a tree—not in the full sun— and allow Mother Nature to rock you in a gentle embrace.

- No matter how busy you are, take time to stop, breathe, and notice all that is happening in nature around you, be it the lazy drone of bees, the intoxicating scent of your neighbor's rose garden, or simply the vibrant blue of the sky above your head.

- Remember how it felt to be a child, when you could play outside all day in the summer? Make room for play and simple enjoyment in your life, whatever your heart calls you to do. Make daisy chains with your children, build wonky sandcastles on the beach, read for hours under a quiet old tree...

- Eat outside whenever possible, and eat simply. In summer our bodies need light, fresh, and easily digested foods, so make a point of adding lots of fruit, vegetables, and aromatic herbs to your meals.

- Unplug from your phone, computer, and social media for at least a good portion of your day: the world will continue without you, I promise, and you will have a chance to rest and replenish your energy without constant input from external sources.

- Learn to set boundaries and say no, both to people and things that drain your energy. (Actually, this is something many of us need to do every season of the year!) By creating healthy boundaries, we assert our own needs and emotional requirements without denying others theirs and create better relationships all around.

- Think about what it is you are grateful for this summer: people, places, scents, tastes, experiences. Meditate on them, and give thanks for all that is good and positive in your life. This can be very powerful, especially when we are stuck in the rut of feeling sorry for ourselves or as if life is passing us by.

- Start every summer day at sunrise, if possible—burn a candle, light some jasmine or rose incense, and hold a small rose quartz crystal in your hands. (Rose quartz supports emotional healing and clarity, and opens us up to greater love and positivity.) Look out at the brightening sky as it warms the earth, and say: "I know this day will be beautiful, positive, and blessed—not just for me but for all around me on this green and wonderful earth. Love surrounds me, and I give love to myself and all things."

GROW

$\mathcal{T}$he summer garden—is there anything more beautiful and full of natural life than a garden of bright flowers and green leaves, fragrance wafting on a warm breeze, with the gentle song of the birds as a quiet background? The herbal garden is particularly enchanting in the summer months and full of opportunities for gathering and celebrating these wonderful little gifts of nature.

Some Herbs to Know

Rose (Rosa species)

I am not going to provide detailed ideas for growing roses—that is just too large and varied a subject for a book like this. If you would like to start your own rose garden, I suggest buying a good book on the subject; also pay a visit to your local garden center, where you will be able to get much useful advice and help.

Suffice it to say, roses are probably among the most loved and useful flowers in the world, with a history that dates back to antiquity. The delightful, heady scent of the blooms is captured in rose essential oil, which I consider to be an absolutely essential part of any home herbal kit (together with rose water/hydrosol). Not only does rose fragrance lift our mood and create a sense of peace and well-being, but its properties are enormously beneficial in skin-care products and can help to reduce redness and irritation, as well as moisturize very dry or mature skin and reduce the appearance of fine lines or wrinkles.

If you do grow your own roses, especially the older, very fragrant ones, you can use the petals in potpourri or add them to baked goods or sugar. Culinary rose water is also available (it is often used in Middle Eastern, Greek, and Indian cooking); it adds a deliciously fragrant note to desserts and other treats. Rose oil or water is included in many of the recipes in this book with good reason: it is a truly fragrant gift of nature.

Thyme (Thymus vulgaris)

Thyme is actually one of the members of the mint family. There are hundreds of varieties, but the best known are common thyme and lemon thyme (*Thymus citriodorus*), which has become increasingly popular as a culinary herb.

101

Thyme grows very happily in containers or window boxes; it likes well-drained soil and plenty of sun, as it is originally a Mediterranean herb. The plant also needs protection from cold winter winds. It can be grown from cuttings or root divisions in spring or summer; after the pretty little flowers have appeared, keep the plants well-trimmed to encourage growth.

Thyme is a very useful herb in the kitchen and adds its distinctive flavor to dishes like poultry, meat, soups, casseroles, sauces, salad dressings, and vinegar. It is one of the herbs that dries well, retaining its aromatic qualities; it also combines happily with many other herbs and spices, among them sage, parsley, and rosemary.

The many species of thyme have numerous medicinal properties and are, among other things, antiseptic, antifungal, and antiviral. Thyme is useful for digestive problems, as it eases spasms and flatulence. A tea or gargle made with thyme leaves is helpful for sore throats or mouth/gum infections. Thyme essential oil can be added to massage oils or baths to ease infections or sore muscles—however, it should not be used during pregnancy or while breastfeeding.

Thyme was originally considered to be a bringer of courage and clarity of spirit; in medieval times knights would pin a sprig of thyme onto their armor to ensure victory in battle. It was also added to herbal pillows to encourage

peaceful dreams and banish melancholy. Use thyme when you want to be reminded of your innate personal strength and power that gives you the ability to create a life that makes your heart sing!

Geranium (Pelargonium graveolens)

We are all familiar with the bright and beautiful geranium flower, but for the purposes of this book, we are using only scented geraniums, specifically the rose-scented variety, which is native to South Africa and has a truly wonderful fragrance. There are quite a number of scented geranium species, with fragrances ranging from camphor to peppermint to citronella. In my mom's garden in South Africa there was an entire path lined with these plants, and their combined perfume was truly breathtaking on warm summer days. The plants do well in fairly hot, dry, and sunny conditions, where they will become quite large, but they also make excellent houseplants if they are given a bright spot to grow. (For even better results, place them outside for a couple of weeks during the summer months.) In the winter the plants can be cut back by half, which will encourage new growth in the spring; don't overwater, as these plants don't like soggy feet.

Although the intensely fragrant leaves can be added to desserts and baked goods, where they will impart a unique

taste, it is for the essential oil that this beautiful plant is most highly prized. Infusions of the leaves also work well, and they make a fragrant addition to herbal teas.

The oil, which is generally nontoxic and nonirritant, cools, revives, and detoxifies the skin and is helpful for reducing wrinkles and blemishes. It also has powerful emotional effects and is a gentle natural antidepressant, balancing the mood and easing anxiety in both adults and children. It's particularly good for this when added to a massage or bath oil or used in a diffuser or oil burner. However, this herb can affect the hormonal system, so it should not be used during pregnancy.

Cilantro (Coriandrum sativum)

This versatile herb (both leaves and seeds) has many applications, although it is generally used mainly as a culinary herb. However, it was widely considered to confer immortality in ancient times and also was used in love potions, among other uses.

It's an annual that does well in sunny spots with light, well-drained soil; don't plant it until all danger of frost is past. It likes moist soil, but don't overwater the plants. In the later summer months, you will be able to harvest the seeds, which are useful in spicy dishes and baking. Essential oil is also made from the seeds.

104

Highly aromatic, the oil has a long tradition of use in both Chinese and Ayurvedic medicine with its warming effect that helps improve circulatory issues and analgesic properties that relieve stiffness and pain in muscles and joints. It's also uplifting to the spirit and can increase energy levels and reduce apathy. For these purposes, it can be added to massage oils or burnt in a diffuser. (Use with caution when pregnant or breastfeeding.)

The chopped leaves, stems, and roots are all used in various cuisines, especially those of India, China, and Latin America. Use them in spicy dishes, stir fries, and curry pastes. (The leaves should always be added towards the end of cooking time so as to retain their bright color and flavor; they are not successful when dried.) The coriander seeds can be dried or ground fresh; roast them in a hot oven for 10–15 minutes to bring out their rich flavor. Dried seeds are best stored whole and only ground when you need them.

I confess to being totally addicted to cilantro in my kitchen, although I also acknowledge that it can be an acquired taste! Those of us who find the taste of cilantro akin to eating soap or stinkbugs are not just being picky; research has proven there is a natural chemical compound called aldehyde found in cilantro, and individuals who have a variation in their olfactory-receptor genes react differently to this chemical. Apparently, chopping, mincing,

or crushing the leaves breaks down these aldehyde compounds and makes them less offensive. Adding the leaves during the cooking process will also help with this.

Lemon Balm (Melissa officinalis)

A delightful member of the mint family, lemon balm is also known as melissa or bee balm. It's been used for centuries. The ancient Greeks believed that planting it would encourage bees in the garden; its strong lemon-scented leaves also deter garden pests, and it's an excellent companion plant for tomatoes and squash.

It's a hardy perennial, liking a fair bit of sun and plenty of moisture; it grows well in containers and is less likely to become pervasive that way, which is a tendency it shares with other members of the mint family.

It has been used for centuries as a calmative and antidepressant, and to help with problems related to nervous tension or stress, including upset stomachs or indigestion. An infusion of the leaves can be drunk as a tea, and it can also be made into tinctures or added to cream or oils. The essential oil is beautiful added to massage oils, bath oils, and beauty preparations.

Lemon balm leaves are best used fresh since they lose their lemony flavor when they are cooked; add them at the last moment to salads, soups, and cold fish dishes. They

also go very well with creamy cheeses. Herbal vinegar made with lemon balm has a wonderfully fresh aroma and taste and is great in dressings and marinades.

Thyme for the Bees

If you grow thyme in your garden, you are also making a wonderful habitat for bees, who adore this flavorful little herb. Pollinators—which include bees, butterflies, moths, bugs, bats, and hummingbirds—are essential for the life and well-being of our natural world, but sadly they are suffering intensely as a result of damaging changes to the earth such as pollution, chemicals, intensive farming, and global warming. Helping them out wherever possible is a wonderful way to bring even more enchantment to our gardens and also helps to nurture the world at large.

In addition to thyme, these essential little beings are also attracted to herbs and flowers such as lavender, lemon balm, rosemary, nasturtium, borage, chamomile, roses, parsley, and scented geranium.

Just by the by—did you know that ladybugs are a particularly beneficial little insect and are also reputed to be a favorite pet of the faeries? In fact, if you find a red ladybug with seven spots, she has almost certainly been placed there by a good faerie to keep an eye on the garden.

107

SUMMER

A Cook's Window Box

If you love cooking, then a cook's window box is a wonderful thing to have, especially if you don't have a garden or only have limited space; it also makes a beautiful gift for a friend. Just make sure the container you choose has drainage holes in the bottom, covered with small stones or pebbles, and use a good quality potting soil. Choose a small plant of each kind and keep all the plants well-trimmed so that one plant does not start to take over the entire box.

FRENCH HERBS: chives, thyme, parsley, oregano, and sage

PIZZA AND PASTA: basil, oregano, chilli, flat-leafed parsley, and a cocktail tomato plant

SPICY ASIAN: mint, coriander, lemongrass, holy basil, and chilli

For these ideas, I am indebted to Debora Robertson's *Gifts from the Garden*.

Harvesting Your Herbs

As summer goes on, you will have lots of herbs to harvest, either from your garden, containers, or window boxes. Sometimes we just need to pick a few leaves or stalks to add to tea or the dish we are preparing, but if we need to harvest a bit more, there are a few ways to ensure the plants remain at their optimum flavor and fragrance.

- ◆ It's preferable to pick your herbs on a dry, sunny day in the late morning or early afternoon, once any dew has evaporated from the leaves, which might turn them moldy.

- ◆ The leaves of annual plants should be harvested just before flowering, while perennial leaves can be harvested anytime. Never pick leaves from a very young plant or one that is not growing well; they should only be picked from mature, well-established plants, as then the active ingredients such as fragrance oils will be at their best.

- ◆ Flowers should be harvested just as they are coming open, not once they are past their peak.

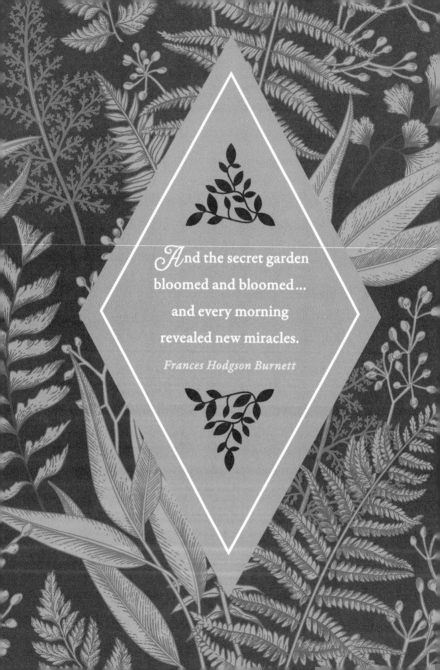

*A*nd the secret garden
bloomed and bloomed...
and every morning
revealed new miracles.

Frances Hodgson Burnett

- Most roots are best harvested in fall, once the plant is past its summer growth period; the exception to this are dandelion roots, which should be harvested in spring.

- For seed heads, cut them off with a length of stalk attached; the seeds can then be shaken out and stored in small jars until dried.

- Fresh herbs can be stored standing upright in a cool place, in a glass jar half filled with fresh water. In this way they should stay green and fragrant for several days.

The quote on the opposite page comes from *The Secret Garden*, the famous book by Frances Hodgson Burnett, which was written in the nineteenth century but remains as fresh and relevant today as then, reminding us of the miracles that are waiting to be created and cultivated in our lives. It all begins with simply stepping outside and opening our eyes!

The Green Art of Foraging

In recent years, the art of foraging or wildcrafting has enjoyed an enormous rise in popularity, as so many people are seeking to find their way back to a wilder, more natural way of living, eating, and creating. Particularly in summer, this is a wonderful way to deepen our connection with our mother the earth, but there are a few simple rules to follow.

Firstly, make sure you know what it is you are harvesting. Plants can often look very similar to the naked eye, and while one plant may be beneficial, another similar one can be quite poisonous or even deadly—Mother Nature can pack quite a punch! As the first step on your foraging journey, invest in a good wild plant identification book for your geographical area.

Be careful where you pick your plants, and if the plants are on private property, ask permission first. (If the answer is no, walk away gracefully.) On areas of public land there are also rules to be followed depending on your area, city, or town.

Never take more than a small quantity of plant material from any given plant, and NEVER rip a plant out by its roots. If the plant seems to be unhealthy or small, leave it alone so that it has a better chance to thrive. And please remember to say thank you to the plants you harvest for their gift.

It's wise to avoid plants growing in possibly polluted areas altogether since they may contain or be coated with potentially harmful toxins. These areas include the sides of major roads and freeways, industrial areas, and bodies of obviously polluted or stagnant water.

Ensure your own safety when foraging in remote areas: dress appropriately, preferably go in pairs or a group, and make sure you have phone contact in case of emergencies, as well as letting someone know where you are going and when you expect to be back.

Taste

The herbal kitchen in summer is full of fresh tastes reflecting the bounty and abundance of the season. In the summer we don't want to spend hours in the kitchen, so fairly quick and easy recipes, many of which can be served cold or at room temperature, as well as being light and digestible, are always welcome.

Magic Green Salt

In moderation, of course, salt is essential for our bodies and health; it's such a wonderful flavor enhancer and also has mystical protective properties, guarding against ill will and trouble. I used to buy all sorts of commercial flavoring salts, but now I prefer to make my own, which can be used in so many delicious and inventive ways: added to breads and marinades, sprinkled on grilled chicken, fish, or meat, stirred into salad dressings…the list is endless.

1 ounce fresh cilantro (leaves and stems)
2 peeled garlic cloves, crushed

1 cup non-iodized sea salt

2 small green chillies, sliced

Zest and juice of 1 large lemon

Roughly chop the cilantro and place in a food processor; add the rest of the ingredients and blitz the mixture until the herbs, garlic, and chillies are finely chopped. Place in a glass jar with a tight-fitting lid and store in the fridge; it lasts a long time! To make a delicious wet rub or basting sauce for meat or chicken, mix 1 tablespoon salt with 1 tablespoon fresh lemon juice and 2 tablespoons olive oil.

Other Salty Ideas

ORIENTAL MAGIC SALT: Use lime zest in place of the lemon and add a small piece of peeled ginger and some chopped lemongrass to the mixture before blending.

CHILLI SALT: Great for grilling! Use fresh oregano instead of cilantro and add 1 tablespoon each black pepper, ground cumin, and smoked paprika.

SEL DU PROVENCE: Omit the chillies and use equal parts fresh rosemary and thyme leaves in place of the cilantro. Add 1 tablespoon each dried oregano, mint, and crumbled dried lavender blossoms, as well as the zest of an orange. This salt is perfect with fish, chicken, or vegetable dishes.

Xipister Sauce

A strange name—but a delicious and versatile sauce from the Basque region of France. Basically, it's an herbal vinaigrette that can be used just about anywhere: on salads, grilled chicken, fish, or steak, drizzled over vegetables, or as a dipping sauce for bread. It's also very easy to make and is a wonderful kitchen gift; the recipe can be increased as needed.

Using a glass jar or bottle with at least 1-pint capacity, pour in 1½ cups white wine vinegar and ½ cup olive oil. Add a few sprigs of fresh rosemary and thyme, 1 bay leaf, the zest of one lemon (cut into thin strips), 2–3 crushed garlic cloves, and 1 or 2 hot chilli peppers cut into slices. Make sure all of these are pushed down well into the vinegar/oil mixture, put the lid on the jar or bottle, and shake very well. Leave in a cool, dark cupboard for at least a week before using. Shake again before each use; the sauce will last for a few months, and the flavor gets stronger and more pronounced over time.

Cucumber and Cilantro Gazpacho

MAKES 4 SERVINGS

The traditional version of this chilled Spanish soup uses flat-leafed parsley, basil, or oregano, but I think the cilantro works really well with the spicy, warm flavors of this dish.

> 1 small onion, peeled and chopped
> 2 garlic cloves, peeled and crushed
> 2 tablespoons olive oil
> 2 tomatoes, peeled and chopped
> 2 cups tomato juice
> 2 cups vegetable stock
> 1 tablespoon red wine vinegar
> ½ teaspoon Tabasco (optional)
> 1 chopped red chilli
> 1 small cucumber
> A handful of fresh cilantro
> Freshly ground black pepper

Fry the onion and garlic in the olive oil until soft and golden. Add the tomatoes, tomato juice, and vegetable stock. Heat gently; don't boil. Remove from heat, cool, then pour the liquid into a blender or food processor. Add the vinegar, Tabasco, and chilli. Blend until a thick, smooth liquid is formed. Peel the cucumber and cut into small ribbons. Stir half of this into the soup and chill very well. Serve in small bowls garnished with the remaining

cucumber ribbons, chopped fresh cilantro, and a little freshly ground black pepper to taste.

This soup is traditionally served with crispy croutons. Cut some slices of French bread into cubes and place on a large baking sheet. Sprinkle with olive oil, freshly ground salt, and a little crushed garlic or grated Parmesan cheese; bake in a hot oven, around 400° F, until the cubes of bread are crispy and golden. Watch them carefully, as they go from being just right to being burnt in a matter of minutes!

Greek Oregano and Lemon Chicken

SERVES 4

One of the simplest and most mouth-watering ways to serve chicken, either hot, warm, or cold—it's the perfect dish for a summer night's feast in the garden. Use chicken pieces with skin and bone for greater flavor; I generally use thighs and breasts, which can be cut into smaller pieces if they are very large.

Preheat oven to 375° F.

> **2 pounds fresh chicken pieces**
> **2 tablespoons olive oil**
> **2 large garlic cloves, crushed**
> **Freshly ground black pepper**
> **½ cup fresh lemon juice**
> **1 cup dry white wine**

2 tablespoons honey

A large handful of fresh oregano

Brown the chicken pieces lightly in the olive oil together with the garlic, then place in a large ovenproof dish and sprinkle with pepper. Mix the lemon juice, wine, and honey together, then pour the mixture evenly over the chicken. Tuck sprigs of oregano between the chicken pieces. Cover the dish and bake for about 45 minutes to 1 hour, then remove the cover and continue cooking until the chicken is browned and the skin crisp. Serve at the temperature you prefer; with a fresh green salad and some good bread, it makes the perfect meal to share.

Caponato al Rosmarino

SERVES 6–8 AS A SIDE DISH

A wonderfully aromatic Italian side dish—my father loved it since it contained all his favorite ingredients: garlic, tomatoes, eggplant, anchovies, and olives. As a child I found the rosemary a little overwhelming, so perhaps it is an acquired adult taste. However, rosemary is a very strong aromatic herb and should always be used in moderation. The anchovies can be left out if preferred.

Preheat oven to 400° F.

2 large eggplants, peeled

2 red onions, peeled and sliced

3 garlic cloves, crushed

1 red pepper, seeded and sliced

2 small green chillis, sliced

2 ripe tomatoes, peeled and chopped finely

½ cup olive oil

4 tablespoons tomato puree

4 chopped anchovy fillets

2 tablespoons capers

2 tablespoons pitted black olives

½ cup dry white wine

1 teaspoon sugar

Freshly ground black pepper to taste

1 tablespoon chopped rosemary

Cut the eggplant into small chunks and place in a large bowl. Add the chopped onions, garlic, red pepper, and chillis, and mix well. Lastly stir in the tomatoes.

In another bowl, mix together the olive oil, tomato puree, anchovy fillets, capers, and olives. Stir in the white wine, sugar, and black pepper to taste. Pour over the eggplant mixture and toss until well coated; spread the vegetables on a large baking sheet lined with foil and sprinkle with rosemary. Bake for 1 hour or until the vegetables are tender and a thickish sauce has formed. (Add more wine, if needed.) Cool slightly and serve. It can also be served

120

chilled as an accompaniment to grilled chicken, fish, or steak. It keeps well in the fridge for a few days.

Tri-Colore Tomato Salad

SERVES 3–4 AS A MEAL OR 6–8 AS A SIDE SALAD

A fresh and delightful summer salad (although the tomatoes are baked first, which gives them greater tenderness and flavor). The robust taste of basil makes it wonderful with Italian and tomato dishes; to ensure none of the aroma and taste are lost, it is best added just before serving.

Preheat oven to 400° F.

20 small, ripe tomatoes
3 tablespoons plus ¼ cup olive oil
1 red onion, thinly sliced
2 garlic cloves, chopped
¼ cup pitted black olives
8 ounces mozzarella cheese
2 tablespoons white wine vinegar
A large handful of torn fresh basil leaves

Slice the tomatoes in half and arrange them in a single layer on a large baking dish. Drizzle with 3 tablespoons olive oil and roast for 30 minutes. Remove from the heat and cool slightly.

Combine the onion and garlic cloves. Arrange the tomatoes on a serving platter and sprinkle with the onion-garlic

121

mixture and the black olives. Tear the cheese into pieces and scatter it on top of the tomatoes. Mix ¼ cup olive oil and white wine vinegar, and use it to dress the salad just before serving. Garnish with the torn basil leaves. Served with good bread and a dry white wine, this makes a good light lunch; it also can be served as a side salad with meat, fish, or pasta dishes.

Lemon-Thyme Snow Cream

MAKES APPROXIMATELY 4 CUPS, OR 4–6 SERVINGS

This is basically a simple frozen yogurt, but the addition of the herbal syrup makes it truly special and a fresh taste sensation for summer! You can swap out mint or lemon balm for the thyme or use lemon thyme if you have it.

>   1 cup water
>   1 cup sugar
>   1 medium lemon, sliced
>   A large handful of fresh thyme leaves
>   2 cups Greek yogurt
>   1½ cups cream
>   Chopped thyme and sliced lemon for garnish

Combine the water, sugar, sliced lemon (pips removed), and thyme leaves in a large saucepan. Simmer until the mixture thickens and is reduced by half. Strain the syrup into a bowl and allow to cool.

122

Place the yogurt in a bowl and stir in ½ cup of the cooled sugar syrup. (The leftovers are wonderful added to teas, cocktails, and the like.) In another bowl, whip the cream to soft peaks and gently fold into the yogurt mixture. Pour into a suitable container and freeze for 1 hour. Remove and beat well to break up any ice crystals. Freeze again until firm. Remove from the fridge at least 15 minutes before serving. Serve in small cups or bowls garnished with a little chopped thyme and thin slice of lemon.

Rose and Lavender Madeleines

MAKES 10–12 MADELEINES

These delicate and buttery little cakes are a true taste of France, and with their gentle floral taste they also bring a little garden magic to the kitchen! You will need a madeleine pan, but they are fairly easy to obtain these days; alternatively, you can use a small muffin pan, but the cakes will not have the traditional shape. Please be sure to use only culinary rose water, which is widely used in both Middle Eastern and Indian cuisine; also use lavender sparingly, otherwise your baked goods can end up tasting like soap! These delicate little cakes make a beautiful addition to a summer tea party, served with cups of Earl Grey tea to which you have added a few crushed lavender blossoms.

Preheat oven to 400° F. Grease a madeleine pan very well and dust lightly with flour.

> **2 eggs**
> **¾ cup plus ¼ cup sugar**
> **¾ cup flour**
> **¼ cup ground almonds**
> **1 teaspoon baking powder**
> **½ stick butter, melted and cooled**
> **2 teaspoons plus 1 teaspoon rose water**
> **1 tablespoon dried lavender**

Beat the eggs and ¾ cup sugar together for at least 5 minutes, until very thick and pale. Then gently fold in the flour, almonds, baking powder and melted butter. Stir in 2 teaspoons rose water and leave the batter to stand for 20 minutes. Bake in the preheated oven for 10–15 minutes, until the cakes are risen and pale gold in color. Cool for 5 minutes, then turn out onto a wire rack to finish cooling.

To make the glaze, combine ¼ cup sugar with 1 teaspoon rose water and enough water to make a thick, pourable glaze. Drizzle the glaze over the madeleines and then sprinkle each with a few crumbled lavender buds. They are best served fresh.

The Herbal Pantry for Summer

At summer's height we can harvest some of her bounty to enjoy—not just for now but as a sweet reminder of summertime once the days start to shorten and grow cool.

Lemon and Herb Oil

MAKES 2 CUPS

This sunny oil captures the true flavor and vibrancy of summer citrus, which is enhanced by the addition of herbs and the spicy warmth of coriander seeds. It's very simple to make and can be used for marinades, salad dressings, or sprinkled over pasta, chicken dishes, and curries.

- **4 large ripe lemons**
- **1 tablespoon fresh rosemary leaves, chopped**
- **1 tablespoon crushed coriander seeds**
- **2 cups olive or peanut oil**

Peel the lemons, then cut the skin into very thin strips. Place the lemon peel in a large sterilized glass jar with a tight-fitting lid. Sprinkle with chopped rosemary and coriander seeds, then pour in the oil. Cover with the lid and leave the jar in a cool, dark place for at least 3 weeks for the flavors to infuse. Then strain the mixture well through a coffee filter and pour the lemon oil into a glass bottle. Seal and use within 3 months.

Olive and Thyme Tapenade

A traditional recipe from the South of France, this delicious olive pâté is wonderful simply spread on slices of toasted country bread, but a little can also be stirred into dips, sauces, and added to fish dishes. Use sun-dried olives or those preserved in oil as olives preserved in brine will make the tapenade too salty. Drain the olives and capers well before mixing up this recipe.

> 2 cups pitted black olives, drained
> 1 tablespoon fresh lemon juice
> 2 tablespoons capers, drained
> 2 cloves crushed garlic
> 5 anchovy fillets (optional)
> 1 tablespoon fresh thyme leaves
> 1 tablespoon brandy
> Approximately ¼ cup olive oil

Combine all the ingredients except for the olive oil in a blender or food processor. Pulse briefly to mix, then gradually add the olive oil; you may not need to use all of it. The mixture should still be fairly chunky. Store the tapenade in

small, sterilized glass jars with tight-fitting lids. Keep in the refrigerator once the jars are opened, where they will keep for up to 3 months.

FALL

Harvest & Celebration

oth spring and fall are seasons of transition, marking shifts between light and darkness, warmth and cold. Fall, in particular, can often be a challenging season for many people, myself included, as it signals the end of the light and warmth of summer and heralds the coming of the frosty winter months. The falling leaves, beautiful though they are in their glorious bright colors, seem a little melancholy as they remind us of things passing and time moving on.

Of course, fall is also a time of harvest and abundance as we gather the fruits of the earth for the darker days ahead with hope and gratitude. Celebration and thanksgiving are also part of this vibrant season, as are the ways in which we remember those who have gone before us on this life journey that we share.

Perhaps, though, the greatest gift of fall is to remind us, in the most natural and beautiful way, that life moves on through cycles and changes, both on this earth and in ourselves. We are no longer the same as we were a few days, months, years ago. And we are not the same as we will be in the future. Just like a leaf or seed pod or ripening fruit, we are designed and destined for change, and fall gently prepares us to accept and let go, like a russet-gold leaf dropping from the branch, so that we can be ready for new blessings and growth.

In this change and transition we can be helped on every level—physical, emotional, and spiritual—by plants, herbs, spices, and other green gifts; we can nourish ourselves both on the inward and outward plane to truly harvest the abundance contained within our soul and spirit.

And suddenly you know:
It's time to start something new
and trust the magic of beginnings.

Meister Eckhart

Heart Notes

Simple blessings and rituals are appropriate for this vibrant season. It's also an intuitive season that can open us up to new awareness and gratitude, not only for the gift that is our lives, but also for all the good things we are given by Mother Earth, our greatest teacher.

Wisdom of the Falling Leaves

This is a simple ritual but one that can be enormously powerful in its changes and effects. Letting go is one of the things so many of us struggle with; we cling on to past events, people, and choices even when it is painfully clear that these attachments are no longer serving us in any positive way (and sometimes never did). The choice to move on is always there for us, but we need to take the first step, and for many of us a specific ritual can be enormously helpful in doing just this.

First, you will need to gather some dry, fallen autumn leaves; they should be fairly large and not too brittle. Alternatively, you can cut leaf shapes out of suitably colored pieces of paper or card stock. With a chalk pencil, on the back of each leaf, write the date and something (or someone) you need to let go of in your life; you don't have to go into great details, just a single word, name, or simple phrase will suffice. I also find it helpful to do this process sitting quietly in a peaceful room or in the garden if it is warm enough, by the light of a few yellow or white candles. You might want to burn a little lavender, sage, or sandalwood incense, too.

Now, place the leaves in a basket—you can do as many as you feel you need—and carry them outside to a place where there is running water: it can be a stream, river, or the ocean. One by one, throw the leaves onto the water, allowing each to be carried away in its turn, and say the following words:

> *Just like the falling leaves, I release you to*
> *the earth and her grace. I no longer choose*
> *to carry this in my life or heart. I am*
> *moving on to new horizons with a sense*
> *of joy, peace, and purpose. And so it is.*

A Gratitude Altar

Gratitude is an important theme in this season of harvest and abundance, for it's a vital part of any truly enchanted or joyful life. We cannot reach our true and happiest potential if we are continually placing a focus on what we *don't* have or our perceived lack in any area, be it practical, financial, or emotional. We often forget the many simple blessings that surround us all day and every day, and creating a gratitude altar is a simple and beautiful way of returning our hearts to this state of awareness.

Altars have been used in all religions and spiritual practices for many centuries as a focus for intention, prayer, and giving thanks. By creating them in our own homes or gardens, we carry on this beautiful tradition in a way that is uniquely meaningful to us.

An altar can be small or large and anywhere you choose to place it: a table, a shelf, the corner of a windowsill. You can cover it with a lovely cloth or leave it bare. Place a candle in the middle of the altar; choose whichever color speaks to you, although I personally choose white as it is the color of upliftment and peace. Add a small vase or glass of fresh herbs or flowers, whatever is in season, particularly if you have grown it yourself or it is a plant that holds meaning for you.

The rest of the gratitude altar is up to you: a seashell from a beach you love, a stone from a favorite garden, feathers from the birds who frequent your green space, a small bowl of salt for positive vibrations and protection. Pictures of those you love and places you have called home, in the truest sense of the word. A few small crystals: rose quartz, amethyst, and turquoise all have healing and psychic properties. Perhaps something to reflect the season's bounty: in fall, a small pumpkin or acorns or a small branch of bright leaves.

I also add a small jar filled with small pieces of paper. Every day I write something I am grateful for in that moment, on that day, and add it to the jar. It's a powerful reminder of just how many blessings we actually do have when we pause to reflect.

Every day light the candle for a few moments and quietly say thank you for blessings already received, blessings in the present moment, and blessings yet to be.

The Journey of Grief

If there is one thing we can all be sure of, we will have to deal with grief at some time in our lives, whether it is the loss of loved ones, friends, and pets or the loss of a long-held dream or hope, something that we realize is never going to happen for us. I am thinking of a dear friend who

135

experienced major grief when she went through an early menopause and realized she would never have a child of her own, something she had always longed for. To some people her grief seemed less real, but I understood it completely.

And perhaps fall is the season when grief seems to be at its most poignant and immediate: Does the earth perhaps also feel grief for the cooling sun, the spent blossoms, the falling leaves? She knows change is both necessary and inevitable, but she honors and mourns the passing of the summer days just the same.

In fall, too, we celebrate many rituals that are closely linked with loss and death: Halloween (All Hallows' Eve), All Saints' and All Souls' days in the Christian calendar, as well as the Día de los Muertos. If, in this vibrant season, you are grieving a loss of any kind, there are gently supportive natural remedies to help you through this difficult time. Please be aware, though, that if grief becomes overwhelming or you find yourself unable to move on with life or find joy in life, there is help out there in the form of counseling, support groups, and the like.

Chamomile essential oil is known for its ability to calm sadness and feelings of loss; burn a little in a diffuser, massage a few drops into your hands, or add the oil to a warm bathtub. Chrysanthemums are used to instill new hope and remind us that nothing truly loved can be lost.

136

Arrange these bright and beautiful blooms wherever you need to feel supported and reassured, or make a flower essence using the flowers (see appendix C) and add some drops to your bathwater or take a few under your tongue.

The Bach flower remedies are known for being supportive in grief and trauma. In particular, Sweet Chestnut is used in times of extreme despair and shock, particularly as a result of bereavement. When my partner died suddenly in an accident a few years ago, I found this remedy very helpful as a support for my fragile emotional state.

Star of Bethlehem is another Bach remedy for grief, shock, and trauma, and it is a key ingredient in the well-known Rescue Remedy. I strongly urge everyone to keep a bottle of Rescue Remedy on hand, as it is truly a miracle worker in times of crisis. It can also be used for accidents and even for animals in times of emotional or physical stress.

Feasting with the Spirits

Food is undoubtedly one of the most powerful ways in which we connect: with ourselves, with others, with the energies of our earth, and with our memories. Who of us does not have certain food memories that can often be triggered by a simple aroma or seeing an old recipe page in a kitchen journal?

Fall is the season when we are, in so many ways, more deeply connected to the spirit world and to those we knew who have already passed through into it. Certain dishes often remind us so clearly (and often poignantly) of those we loved, and still do, for physical death does not remove the emotions of the heart and soul. For me, this time brings many special recipes to mind. Butter chicken curry for my partner James. Tomato and herb pasta sauce—a favorite of my Italian father. Pancakes with lemon and cinnamon syrup—a beloved uncle who was so good to me when I was a little girl. I'm sure everyone can think of similar taste memories like the cookies you made with your mom or the chicken dish you shared on your first visit to Paris.

On either October 31 or November 1 I'd like to suggest we celebrate by feasting with the spirits that are still so very present in our lives. This ritual can be done alone or with others, particularly if you all honor and share memories of a particular person.

Prepare a special recipe. Then spread a beautiful cloth on a table or on the floor. Light several candles, maybe in pink, white, or gold. Place a bunch of sage or rosemary in the middle of the table. Slowly and mindfully enjoy the food you have prepared, perhaps sharing your various memories of the person whose life you are celebrating. Then say the following words, adjusted for who is speaking:

138

I remember you with love, (name). You were a part of my life and thus you remain and always will. May your spirit be with me and bless me this night and as I journey into the future. I celebrate you and your soul always, as I celebrate myself. Blessings and light.

We remember you with love, (name). You were a part of our lives, and thus you remain and always will. May your spirit be with us and bless us this night and as we journey into the future. We celebrate you and your soul always, as we celebrate ourselves. Blessings and light.

Then drink a toast with fresh spring water or a glass of sparkling champagne.

CREATE

*H*erbs, spices, fruits, and flowers—all can be used in fall to create simple, healing body preparations and aromatic products for the home and the heart.

Chakra Herbal Bath Crystals

I have been making various bath crystals and salts for a number of years now, but only recently decided to create a range suitable for use with the seven different chakras of the body. (See page 34 for more details about the essential oils linked to each chakra.) The basic recipe is the same, but different oils are added to each, and also a little natural food coloring. Only a tiny amount, please; one wants to be able to see the individual colors, but not be blinded by them or end up with colored skin and tub! I use a wooden stick to stir in the color very gradually; you can always add a little more, but you can't take it out.

Basic Bath Crystals

This recipe makes 2 cups of bath crystals. Combine 1 cup Epsom salts and ½ cup each non-iodized sea salt and baking soda in a bowl. Stir in the essential oils of your choice and then a few drops of suitable food coloring. Mix very well, then store in glass jars with tight-fitting lids—otherwise the steam and heat of the bathroom will cause the crystals to clump and harden.

Chakra Bath Crystals

ROOT CHAKRA (Red): 10 drops patchouli oil, 6 drops ylang-ylang

SACRAL CHAKRA (Orange): 7 drops each sandalwood and jasmine

SOLAR PLEXUS CHAKRA (Yellow): 8 drops lemon, 6 drops juniper

HEART CHAKRA (Green): 6 drops each geranium, lavender, and rose

THROAT CHAKRA (Blue): 8 drops rosemary, 6 drops peppermint

THIRD EYE CHAKRA (Purple): 7 drops each thyme and lemon

CROWN CHAKRA (White or Indigo): 6 drops each neroli, frankincense, and jasmine

Apple and Sage Clarifying Toner

This is a simple and light toner that helps to balance oily skin and refresh mature, blemished, or dull skin.

Take one large apple and chop it into chunky pieces, discarding the seeds. Place in a saucepan with a handful of fresh sage leaves and cover with ¾ cup distilled or spring water.

Bring to a boil and simmer gently for 15–20 minutes, until the apple is very soft. Allow to cool, then strain very well into a glass bowl. (There should be no pieces of apple or sage leaf in the liquid as this can cause it to form mold.) Stir in 2 tablespoons each witch hazel and apple cider vinegar and ½ teaspoon benzoin tincture. Pour the liquid into suitable sterilized glass bottles and keep in a cool, dark cupboard. To use, apply with a cotton wool pad over the face and neck, avoiding the eyes.

This makes about 1 cup toner, which lasts for 2–3 weeks.

Spicy Chai Skin Scrub

The spices used in chai are wonderfully warming, aromatic, and an excellent addition to beauty products as they have antiaging benefits and are also helpful for blemished skin or acne. You can make your own chai mixture very easily by combining the following dried spices in a small glass

142

jar: 2 tablespoons each ground cinnamon, ginger, and nutmeg, and 1 tablespoon each ground cloves, coriander, and cardamom.

To make a sweet and spicy skin scrub, place 1 cup sugar and ½ cup Epsom salts in a bowl. Stir in 4 tablespoons coconut oil (warmed if it has set) and 1½ teaspoons of the spicy chai blend. Mix well and store in an airtight jar. Scoop out a few handfuls of the scrub and use it on moistened skin, rubbing in circular motions. Rinse off well.

Another alternative is a rooibos skin scrub that is wonderfully clarifying and has antioxidant properties. Make in the same way as above but only use 1 teaspoon of the spicy chai blend plus the contents of 2 rooibos tea bags to the scrub.

Simply Positive
Whipped Body Butter

This body butter not only smells delightful and has wonderful skin-soothing properties, but it also encourages positive, uplifting thoughts and can help ease anxiety or fear.

Melt together 6 tablespoons shea butter, 6 tablespoons cocoa butter, and ½ cup coconut oil in a glass bowl set over a pan of simmering water. When the oils are melted, remove from heat and stir in 2 tablespoons almond oil.

143

Add 8 drops neroli essential oil and 6 drops each frankincense and starflower/borage essential oils. Place in the refrigerator until the mixture is firm, then remove and use a hand mixer to whip it to a fluffy consistency. (This may take some time, but the cream should have the consistency of thick and creamy vanilla frosting when it is done.)

Spoon into small, sterilized glass jars or pots and store in a cool place. Use abundantly to moisturize the body or as a nighttime cream.

Reviving Bath Elixir

This simple recipe is wonderful for those early fall nights when you feel tired and lethargic after a busy day and need to give yourself an emotional boost.

To a ¼ cup of almond or jojoba oil, add 6 drops each sweet orange and rosemary essential oils and 4 drops lemon balm oil. Store in a small dark glass bottle and add a few drops to your bathtub or diffuser.

Simmering Spirit Potpourri

We are all familiar with potpourri, that scented mix of flowers and herbs that has been used for centuries to add fragrance and freshness to our living spaces. However, although I used to make my own potpourri, it uses a great deal of plant material, so now I prefer to use a simpler and

easier method: simmering potpourri. This fragrant mix has the potential to completely change the energy of a space, especially when we are feeling negative or caught up in less-than-ideal situations. These scents will not only create a wonderful aroma throughout your home but will aid in protecting and invigorating the spirit.

Fill a large pan with at least 1½ pints spring or distilled water. Add the following to the water: several sprigs of fresh rosemary, a handful of bay leaves, 1 thinly sliced orange, and 2 cinnamon sticks. Then add 5 drops of essential oil: good ones to choose are lemon, rosemary, sage, or frankincense, as all of these oils have uplifting and protective qualities.

Allow to simmer very gently so that the rising steam gently fragrances the air while being careful to ensure that the water does not boil away. This is a particularly good ritual before any kind of gathering in your home or when you wish to feel a little closer to the spirit world.

After use, allow the liquid to get completely cold, then strain it and pour it into a plastic spray bottle to be used as a simple room or space mist.

NURTURE

*A*s we prepare for darker and colder days, we can also take advantage of fall's gifts to prepare ourselves both physically and emotionally for these changes so that we can truly embrace the magic of the waning year.

Ginger and Rosemary Massage Oil

Ginger is known for its powerful healing properties on many levels. This aromatic and warming massage oil has strong anti-inflammatory properties, especially when coupled with rosemary, and is particularly helpful for painful joints and muscles, which often start to become more problematic as the weather cools down. This oil also helps improve circulation, but it is strong and potentially irritating for some skin, so should be used in moderation. (If in doubt, do a small patch test on your skin first.)

To make a small bottle of oil, mix together 2 tablespoons almond oil with 8 drops ginger essential oil and 4 drops rosemary essential oil. Store in a small, sterilized dark glass bottle; apply a few drops directly to the affected areas or add a few drops to a warm bathtub. The oil keeps for 3 months.

Nurturing and Calming
Aura/Room Mist

This light and fragranced mist can be used as a light body or room spray—anywhere you need to reduce stress and anxiety and create a calming atmosphere for letting go and moving forward. Vetiver is an essential oil particularly helpful for this, as is the old favorite, lavender. Clary sage is also a calming, stress-relieving fragrance.

Mix ½ cup each rose water and distilled water in a bowl, then whisk in 2 tablespoons aloe vera gel until it has dissolved. (If you don't have aloe vera gel, you can just use additional distilled water.) Then add 2 tablespoons witch hazel and 1 tablespoon vegetable glycerin. Stir well before adding 10 drops vetiver, 6 drops lavender, and 5 drops clary sage essential oils. Pour into a sterilized glass spray bottle and store in a cool, dark cupboard. It will keep well for up to 6 months.

Two Tonics for Fall

In fall we need to start preparing ourselves both physically and mentally for the long months of dark and cold that lie ahead, ensuring we will be able to meet the challenges of winter with heart and spirit. Fortunately, there are many simple herbal tonics that can give us this important boost on every level, and they taste great as well.

A Thyme, Honey, and Lemon Tonic

Based on a traditional oxymel, this is both delicious and enormously helpful taken on a regular basis during fall; this is especially effective if you are feeling particularly debilitated, tired, or as if you have a cold coming on. To make this tonic even more potent, you can add a few peeled garlic cloves or a little chopped horseradish to the jar—although the latter is definitely more of an acquired taste for those who really like to up the heat factor.

Place a very large handful of fresh thyme leaves (or 1 cup dried leaves) in a large glass jar. Add 1 thinly sliced lemon (pips removed), then pour in 1 cup of apple cider vinegar and 1 cup raw honey. Shake the jar very well, seal it, and place on a cool, dark shelf for 2–3 weeks, shaking the jar every day. Strain the mixture very well through cheesecloth or a large coffee filter. Clean and sterilize the jar before storing the tonic in it. Kept in the fridge, it lasts for several months, and you can take a few tablespoons on a daily basis. Makes about 2 cups of tonic.

Inspired Connections Tonic

A friend of mine swears by this wine-based tonic for gaining greater strength, clarity, insight, and even prophetic powers. I recommend using a fairly strong sweet red wine or even a port for this; however, if you prefer less sweetness, a dry red wine or sherry also tastes good. You can also add different herbs, according to your taste; lavender and thyme work well with the wine.

Crush about 10 black peppercorns in a mortar and pestle, then place in a large glass jar. Add ¼ cup each of dried rosemary, basil, and sage leaves. Pour in 1 bottle of red wine, port, or sherry. Seal the jar and stand in a cool cupboard for 2 weeks, shaking occasionally. Strain the tonic wine back into the bottle, replace the cork or cap, and enjoy a small glass at night before bedtime.

Marigold Healing Lotion

This gentle yet healing lotion is infused with the magic of calendula, which has both antiseptic and anti-inflammatory properties and can be applied to wounds, cuts, eczema, sunburns, inflamed skin, or minor burns. Don't use on deep wounds, though, since it causes rapid healing, and this might close the infection inside the wound.

Place a handful of fresh marigold petals and/or leaves in a small saucepan and cover with ¾ cup spring water. Bring to a boil, simmer for 10 minutes, then remove from heat and allow to cool and infuse for a few hours. In a small bowl set over a pan of simmering water, place ½ cup sweet almond or jojoba oil and 1 tablespoon grated beeswax or beeswax pellets. Warm very gently until the beeswax has melted. Stir in 1 tablespoon honey and cool slightly before adding the strained marigold infusion and ¼ teaspoon benzoin tincture. Mix well to form a smooth lotion, then pour into small sterilized bottles or jars. Best kept in the refrigerator, where it will last for several weeks.

Lavender and Rosemary Vinegar

This sounds rather like something that should be in the taste section—and in fact a few teaspoons of this vinegar add a wonderfully green/floral note to salad dressings,

marinades, and sauces—but vinegar has so many uses for health and healing that this is a useful mixture to keep on hand at all times. I certainly am never without it in my herbal apothecary.

Place 1 large handful each fresh lavender leaves/blossoms and rosemary stalks in a large glass jar and pour over enough apple cider vinegar to cover the plant material completely. Leave in a cool, dark place for at least a week, shaking well every day. Then strain the mixture very well and pour the flavored vinegar into a glass bottle with a good seal. Keep in a cool, dark cupboard.

Some ideas for using it are:

- for any irritated or scalded areas of skin, use a little of the vinegar on a damp cotton wool pad (avoiding broken skin or the eye area)

- to deodorize and refresh the skin, add a few drops to bathwater

- to cleanse and refresh sore, tired feet, add to foot baths

- to make hair shiny and healthy, use a little in your final hair rinse (this mixture also works well for keeping the dark tones of brown hair vibrant; for a rinse for light hair, replace the rosemary with chamomile blossoms; for gray hair, sage is good)

Sweet Lips Salve

Cinnamon is such a wonderful scent, full of nostalgia for many of us as it recalls days in the kitchen and wonderful things baking in the oven! It's also a truly versatile spice with antibacterial and antifungal properties, which makes it perfect for this simple lip salve that you can carry with you and simply apply anytime you need to moisturize and rejuvenate your lips.

In a small glass bowl over simmering water, melt together 3 tablespoons almond oil and 2 teaspoons beeswax flakes. Remove from the heat and stir in the contents of a vitamin E oil capsule and 6 drops cinnamon essential oil. Pour into tiny pots or jars and keep cool.

Coconut Turmeric Latte

This soothing and restorative drink is particularly good just before bedtime, as it will settle and calm you in preparation for a peaceful night's sleep. If you don't like coconut milk, you can use another nut milk, such as almond, or even regular dairy milk.

To make 1 cup, combine 1 cup coconut milk, 1 tablespoon ground turmeric, and ½ teaspoon ground ginger and gently warm without boiling. Stir in 1 teaspoon honey and serve.

Chai Spice Blend

Easy to whip up, this warming and restorative blend can be added to so many things: a cup of black or green tea, baked goods, bathtime treats like salts and scrubs, and more.

Simply mix together 2 tablespoons each ground cinnamon, ginger, and nutmeg, and 1 tablespoon each ground cloves, coriander, and cardamom. Store in a small, airtight jar and use as needed. You can also cut small squares of muslin or cheesecloth and place a tablespoon of the mix in the middle of each before tying it up into a ball with cotton string or twine. These spice balls can be dropped into tea blends, chutney mixtures, and also used to infuse oil or vinegar—in which case you can simply add a few spoons of the spice to the liquid.

Simple Ways to Nurture Your Spirit in the Fall

Gratitude is a key theme in the fall: gratitude for the abundance of life all around us and gratitude for the many gifts we have on an individual basis. A few moments spent in the morning or evening quietly reflecting on our blessings is a peaceful way to focus on positivity that also ensures greater joy and prosperity in the future.

- Catch a few falling leaves and bring them into your home; arrange them in a bowl or small jug. They represent Mother Nature's ongoing gifts to us and are a symbol of luck and protection.

- If you are grieving for someone who has passed on or simply moved away from your life, please allow yourself to feel that sadness. Honor it. Don't feel you have to be strong or pretend to be happy all the time; that is neither helpful nor healthy. Spend time alone with the memories— light a candle, burn a little frankincense or sandalwood—and be still. Remember the person, hold them with love in your heart, and then gently let them go.

- As the weather starts to cool down, warm yourself up from the inside out. Swap out summer bedclothes for warmer blankets or soft quilts, buy or knit a new soft sweater in a vibrant shade, get some fluffy socks for bedtime.

- Harvest herbs and turn them into flavorful reminders of the summer's bounty that will warm the chilly winter months.

154

- Start enjoying some of the fruits of the harvest time like root vegetables, apples, and, of course, pumpkin! Add spices to your kitchen magic, lots of them—just like herbs, they are full of wonderful health and taste benefits. And remember how delicious warming soups and baked treats can be in your fall menus.

- Fall is a time of letting go with gentleness and grace. To this end, think about what you need or want to say no to in your life. It's often not easy to change the status quo, but ultimately it needs to be done for your own personal growth and happiness.

- Build a bonfire outdoors (following appropriate safety rules) and revel in the light and warmth echoing the brilliance of the fading sun.

- Make a mixture of the following essential oils: 5 drops rosemary, 5 drops sage, and 3 drops pine. Add to a spray bottle filled with ½ cup each witch hazel and spring water. Use to bring clarity, harmony, and protection to the rooms of your home.

GROW

*F*all is a busy and bountiful time for Mother Earth as she shares her many wonderful gifts with us in the form of seeds, flowers, spices, and fruits, all of which can be used to create greater health and abundance on every level.

Some Herbs to Know

Sage (Salvia officinalis)

This is probably one of the most loved and useful herbs, both in the kitchen and herbal apothecary. There are over a thousand species of sage, but common sage is the one we most grow and use, with its fresh, slightly woody fragrance. It's an evergreen or woody perennial plant that can become quite large; however, it's also an excellent choice for a potted herb garden, provided it gets plenty of sun and is cut back well in the fall. Sage doesn't like frost, so to ensure plenty of fresh herbs over the cooler months, bring it into a warm kitchen spot in the winter.

Sage is a stimulating, antiseptic, and calmative herb. It's excellent for dealing with frayed nerves and mental exhaustion, especially when sipped as a tea. It's also helpful for respiratory problems, digestive issues, sore and inflamed joints, and as a gargle for sore throats or bad breath.

However, sage has properties far beyond the immediate physical realm: white sage is used in many sacred ceremonies by Native Americans and is also an important part of other cultural practices. (It's important to note that common sage can also be used for these rituals if you can't access white sage.) Sage helps us to clear away stagnant or negative energies from both ourselves and our living spaces, and it is also highly protective, offering us greater awareness and insight as we move forward while at the same time making us aware of blocks and potential dangers on the path.

Of course, we all know and (mostly) love sage as a savory addition to stuffings, sauces, and more; it dries well and retains much of its flavor but can also be used fresh, either chopped and added to turkey or chicken recipes. The fresh leaves can be fried until crisp in a little olive oil and then sprinkled over dishes such as pasta or grilled meat and poultry. It also has a wonderful affinity with cheese.

Basil (Ocimum basilicum)

This aromatic plant, synonymous with the foods of the Mediterranean, is a tender annual that needs both sunshine and shelter to thrive in the garden. Seeds are sown in late spring; the plants need to be kept well-trimmed to ensure plenty of bushy growth. Once the cooler days of fall start, it's a good idea to bring the basil inside and keep it in pots in the kitchen area so that you will have a plentiful supply of this delightful herb through winter. It isn't possible to grow basil year-round in certain climates, even indoors, as it comes from warm climates. In that case, one needs to have a good supply of dried basil gathered during the summer months!

There are many varieties of basil, some more compact than others and suitable for containers and hanging baskets. Tulsi, or holy basil, is a beautiful variety with wonderful long, slightly purple leaves; this plant is considered sacred in many Eastern cultures and is used extensively in various medicinal and spiritual practices such as Ayurveda.

Of course, basil is delicious used in the kitchen and pairs particularly well with tomato-based dishes and vegetables and salads in general. Like sage, it dries well and does retain much of its vibrant flavor, but generally it is best to use the fresh leaves towards the end of the cooking process or to scatter them on salads and cold dishes.

It's a refreshing and calmative herb, while at the same time also restoring energy and helping with fatigue. Basil can be used to address issues like aches and pains in the body, colds and flu, and indigestion. Basil essential oil can be used in skin preparations, where it helps clarify, refresh, and tone the skin, especially when it is prone to irritation and breakouts. The oil can be burnt in a diffuser or a few drops added to a candle to ease headaches and general tiredness, but the oil should be avoided when pregnant or breastfeeding and not be used on young children.

Calendula (Calendula officinalis)

This bright, sunny member of the daisy family has been around for thousands of years; the ancient Egyptians swore by its oil as a healing and antiaging remedy! More commonly known as marigold, it's an easy addition to any garden and also grows happily in containers; seeds should be sown in spring and will self-seed again in late summer or early fall, ensuring plenty of blooms the following year. These plants like rich, well-drained soil and lots of sun but not too much water.

Marigold is wonderful planted in large groups in a garden, as its flowers attract bees and other beneficial insects while also deterring leaf-eating bugs. It can be used for both medicinal and culinary applications, and the flowers

and leaves can also be dried. An infusion of marigold petals or leaves can be added to skincare preparations for acne or dry, irritated, or aging skin. It's an excellent anti-inflammatory and healing plant that is often added to wound treatments. The essential oil is helpful for stress, tension, and anxiety, and it can be used in massage oils or added to bathwater. Please note that calendula should not be taken internally while pregnant or breastfeeding.

The petals of marigold flowers, either dried or fresh, can be added to salads or sprinkled on cold dishes for a summery burst of color. They add a spicy note not unlike saffron but a lot less expensive and more accessible.

Ginger (Zingiber officinale)

Not just a favorite spice in the kitchen, with its wonderful warm and aromatic taste, ginger has numerous health benefits which have been proven over many centuries of use. Ginger is excellent at soothing nausea and digestive upsets, and it can be wonderfully effective at healing (or warding off) colds and flu. As the year goes on and we start to become a little overwhelmed by the demands of the upcoming holiday season, ginger can help ease fatigue and clarify thinking.

It is possible to grow ginger in your garden, but I find it easier to buy the fresh roots at local farmers' markets.

Choose fairly young ginger roots, which are thinner and less fibrous. The whole root can be stored in a paper bag for a few days, or alternatively you can peel, grate, or slice it finely, and store in a jar in the fridge for a few weeks. Obviously ground ginger is widely available and makes a handy kitchen standby if you can't access fresh, but please do check that it is still highly fragrant before using it!

Turmeric (Curcuma longa)

Many of us are mostly familiar with turmeric as a culinary spice, specifically for use in curry dishes and pickles/chutneys, but it is actually a medicinal spice of note that has been used in Indian and Chinese cultures for centuries to treat ailments such as arthritis, stomach disorders, diabetes, allergies, dementia, and cardiovascular problems. We are finally catching up with this knowledge. Its use has become far more widespread in recent years, with turmeric being taken as a dietary supplement, added to teas, and even included in some skincare preparations.

We can buy turmeric root in its ground form very easily, but fortunately the fresh roots are also becoming more widely available and can often be found at organic markets or Eastern food stores. The fresh root can be grated or sliced thinly; it can also be added to curry pastes. However, be sure to wear gloves when handling turmeric root as it

is also a powerful dye—and you will end up with bright yellow hands! It can be added in limited quantities to skin preparations, but I prefer to use it as a tea or culinary herb.

Planting an Astrological Garden

We are all familiar with the twelve astrological signs, with each of us linked to one of these through our day of birth. But what we may not be so familiar with is the fact that each sun or moon sign is also associated with certain flowers and herbs. As long ago as the seventeenth century, the English herbalist Nicolas Culpeper proposed there was a link between certain herbs and flowers and the heavenly bodies and suggested it was effective to use these selected plants to treat people born under that particular astrological sign.

It can be intriguing and rewarding to develop small (or large) herb and flower gardens devoted to one or more of the astrological signs. You could also make a small container garden or window box using some of the suggested plants. Another lovely idea I have used is to create individual fragrant oils using essential oils based on the ideas given below. This makes a truly beautiful and inspiring gift.

ARIES: bergamot, carnation, cumin, fennel, rosemary

TAURUS: apple, daisy, magnolia, patchouli, rose, thyme

GEMINI: bergamot, dill, lavender, lily, parsley, vervain

CANCER: lemon balm, jasmine, rose, sandalwood

LEO: chamomile, cinnamon, marigold, nutmeg, sweet orange

VIRGO: lavender, mint, patchouli, thyme, verbena

LIBRA: marjoram, sandalwood, spearmint, thyme, violet

SCORPIO: basil, cumin, ginger, myrrh, sandalwood

SAGITTARIUS: anise, cedarwood, orange, sage, ylang-ylang

CAPRICORN: cinnamon, comfrey, lemon thyme, mimosa, patchouli, vetiver

AQUARIUS: cedarwood, cypress, lavender, mint, pine

PISCES: jasmine, lemon, neroli, sweet pea

An Herbal Pantry

Can there be anything nicer than having an herbal pantry, one filled with all good and fragrant gifts from the earth, as the year grows ancient and we yearn for warmth and comfort? It's possible to have your very own herbal culinary and medicinal store, no matter how small your living space. All you need is a few shelves in a cupboard (preferably one with doors so that light and heat do not penetrate).

To start with, plan on drying your own herbs, perhaps using bounty gathered from your own garden. I know it's very easy to simply buy dried herbs at the store, but somehow they seem to have so much more energy and taste when you dry your own. Because I have limited space, I use large flat baskets lined with kitchen towels to dry my herbs. I check that the leaves are dry, without any dew or rain, and remove any withered or damaged ones, then spread them out in the baskets, which are placed on top of the kitchen cupboards. The drying process will take a few days to a week, depending on the warmth and humidity of the space.

If you have more space, consider drying herbs in bunches—on quilt or laundry racks or suspended from a clothesline.

Simply make small bundles of each herb, tie firmly with cotton twine, and hang up to dry. Again, this process should not take more than a week.

Then the herbs can be crumbled or packed whole into small glass jars, preferably dark glass ones with airtight lids. Clearly label and date each jar, as one kind of herb can look a lot like another; it's wise to check your herb jars regularly, at least every six months or so, and if you find ones that have lost their aroma or are showing signs of mold, be ruthless and throw them away.

Herbs and flowers that are particularly easy and useful to dry include:

- scented geranium leaves
- lavender (blossoms and leaves)
- bay leaves
- marigold flowers
- roses
- chamomile (flowers and leaves)
- lemon balm and lemon verbena leaves
- mint
- rosemary sprigs
- sage leaves
- thyme

TASTE

*I*n the fall we leave the lighter foods and tastes of spring and summer behind and turn to more warming, aromatic dishes that will nourish us for the winter ahead. We also find kitchen magic in using the many gifts of the harvest in creative and delicious ways.

Pumpkin Fritters with Sage

MAKES 25–30 SMALL FRITTERS

Pumpkin fritters are enormously popular in South Africa, where I grew up. They are served as a side dish, with grills and barbecues, and simply eaten out of hand as a snack. And they make a wonderful treat for Halloween! The sage is my addition as they are normally made just with cinnamon, but I find the sage and pumpkin a delicious combination. I prefer to use pumpkin I have cooked, drained, and mashed myself, but you can use canned pumpkin too.

2 cups puréed pumpkin

2 teaspoons brown sugar

2 eggs

1 cup cake flour

2 teaspoons baking powder

½ teaspoon salt

1 tablespoon crumbled dried sage

Vegetable oil for frying

Mixture of brown sugar/cinnamon (optional)

In a large bowl, mix together the pumpkin, sugar, eggs, cake flour, baking powder, and salt to make a thick, smooth batter that drops from a spoon. Then stir in the sage; you can also use a few small fresh leaves, finely chopped, if you prefer.

In a heavy frying pan, heat about ⅓ inch vegetable oil until hot, then drop tablespoonfuls of the pumpkin batter into the oil—don't overcrowd the pan. After a few minutes, turn the fritters over gently and cook on the other side until both sides are crispy and golden brown, with no raw batter remaining inside. Drain very well on kitchen towels and keep warm until serving. You can sprinkle them with a mixture of brown sugar and cinnamon before serving.

Fireside Mushroom Soup

This is based on a traditional French recipe and is the perfect soup for fall—warming and flavorful to enjoy around a cozy fire as darkness falls outside. Thyme is used in this soup as it pairs beautifully with both mushrooms and onions. A bowl of this soup and you will feel both energized and comforted. You can use any mushrooms, either white, brown, or wild, or a combination of all three.

> ½ stick butter
>
> 3 tablespoons olive oil
>
> 3 large onions, thinly sliced
>
> ½ pound mushrooms, sliced
>
> 3 peeled and chopped garlic cloves
>
> 2 cups chicken broth
>
> 1½ cups dry red wine
>
> A handful of fresh thyme sprigs
>
> 2 bay leaves
>
> Salt and pepper to taste

Heat the butter and olive oil in a large soup pot over medium heat, add the onions and cook gently for at least 20 minutes, until they are soft and golden. Stir in the mushrooms and garlic, and continue cooking for another 15 minutes. Then add the broth, wine, thyme, and bay leaves, as well as salt and freshly ground black pepper to

taste. Bring to a boil, then reduce the heat and simmer for at least 45 minutes.

Before serving, remove the thyme sprigs and bay leaves. Warm soup bowls and divide the soup between them. This is delicious served with slices of crusty French bread and cheese such as Camembert or Havarti.

Harvest Lamb Casserole

SERVES 4–6

Fall is the perfect time to enjoy hearty casseroles, and this recipe is a delicious meal-in-one-pot—all you need to add is a fresh side salad and a glass of good wine. If you don't want to use lamb, beef works well, too.

Preheat oven to 350° F.

- **2 pounds boneless lamb, cubed**
- **2 tablespoons seasoned flour (add 1 teaspoon dried herbs and a little salt and freshly ground black pepper to the flour)**
- **4 tablespoons olive oil**
- **2 medium onions, sliced thinly**
- **3 garlic cloves, peeled and crushed**
- **2 cups lamb or chicken broth**
- **1 cup dry white wine**
- **1 tablespoon tomato puree**
- **½ pound small potatoes**
- **3 sprigs fresh rosemary**

169

Zest of ½ a lemon

Chopped fresh parsley

Coat the meat in the seasoned flour and keep aside. In a large Dutch oven heat the olive oil, then add the onions and garlic and fry for 10 minutes until softened. Add the meat cubes and brown lightly. Then pour in the broth, wine, and tomato puree, cover, and cook for 1 hour. Cut the potatoes in half (no need to peel them) and add to the casserole, together with the fresh rosemary.

Continue cooking until the potatoes are soft and the meat tender. Sprinkle with the lemon zest and chopped parsley, and serve the dish piping hot.

Spicy Coconut Chicken

SERVES 4–6

This aromatic and warming chicken dish is not unlike Thai red curry, but it's a little less hot. (You can add a few extra red chillies if you want to increase the heat factor.) The paste is easy to make, either in a blender or mortar and pestle, and keeps well in the refrigerator if you don't use it all.

Spice Paste

2 garlic cloves, crushed

1 teaspoon cumin seeds

2 small red chillies, sliced

2 tablespoons chopped cilantro

170

1 teaspoon ground turmeric

1 teaspoon ground ginger

1 teaspoon ground coriander

Zest and juice of 1 lime

Mix all the ingredients together well to form a slightly chunky paste.

Add a little oil to a large skillet, Dutch oven, or wok.

Vegetable oil

1 chicken, cut into serving pieces

5 shallots, thinly sliced

1 cup coconut cream (or milk)

1 cup chicken broth

Add the spice paste to the oil and fry the chicken pieces and shallots until golden. Pour in the coconut cream and broth and simmer gently until the chicken is soft and the sauce has thickened. Serve with lots of fragrant steamed jasmine or basmati rice and extra cilantro and chillies.

Creamy Roots Bake

SERVES 6–8 AS A SIDE DISH

Root vegetables are such an intrinsic part of fall, and they bring us such nourishing and grounding energy that we should make as much use of them as possible! This simple but flavorful dish is wonderful served as an accompaniment to roasts and casseroles, but it also makes a great

171

vegetarian main dish. (You can also use half sweet potatoes and half regular potatoes if you prefer.)

Preheat oven to 350° F and butter a deep, large baking dish well.

6–8 potatoes, peeled and sliced

2 large carrots, peeled and sliced

1 large onion, sliced

1 cup heavy cream

1 cup milk

1 teaspoon dried thyme

½ teaspoon dried rosemary

Salt and pepper to taste

4 ounces feta cheese, crumbled

2 tablespoons grated Parmesan

Fresh thyme sprigs to garnish (optional)

Boil the potatoes and carrots in lightly salted water for 10 minutes. Drain, cool, and mix with the sliced onion. Spread the vegetables out evenly in the prepared baking dish. Beat together the cream, milk, dried herbs, salt, and pepper, then pour this mixture over the vegetables, making sure they are covered by the liquid. Cover the dish and bake for 45 minutes; the vegetables should be soft and the liquid reduced somewhat.

Remove the cover, sprinkle the crumbled feta and Parmesan over the vegetables, and return to the oven for

another 25 minutes. The cheese should be melted and the vegetable bake golden brown. Sprinkle with some fresh thyme sprigs, if desired, and serve straightaway.

Apple Cinnamon Dessert Cake

MAKES 9 SQUARES OF CAKE

Apples and cinnamon are a fall match made in heaven, and this simple cake is wonderful as a simple, comforting kind of dessert.

Preheat oven to 350° F and grease an 8- or 9-inch square baking pan well.

1 cup sugar
½ stick butter, softened
2 eggs
1½ cups flour
2 teaspoons baking powder
½ teaspoon salt
2 teaspoons ground cinnamon
⅓ cup milk
3 apples, peeled and chopped
1 teaspoon vanilla extract

Cream the sugar and butter together until light and fluffy. Beat in the eggs. Sift together the flour, baking powder, salt and cinnamon, and add to the butter mixture alternately with the milk to form a smooth batter. Stir in the

chopped apples and vanilla extract. Spread the batter in the baking pan and bake for 20 minutes, until just pale golden.

Sauce

1 stick butter

1 cup single cream

½ cup dark brown sugar

½ teaspoon vanilla extract

While the cake bakes, prepare the sauce by melting together butter, cream, sugar, and vanilla. Don't allow the mixture to boil. Remove the cake from the oven and carefully pour the warm sauce over the top. Return to the oven for another 10 minutes, then remove and cool in the pan. Serve warm cut into squares and with a little more cream on the side.

The Herbal Pantry: Herb Jellies

Herb jellies are one of the nicest ways I know of preserving the magic of herbs for use through the fall and winter months. They can be used in so many ways: as a topping for baked goods, added to sauces and marinades, or brushed

onto chicken and other meats before cooking. There are really no limits to the herbs you can use, either singly or in combination. Other extras you can add are a few sliced red or green chillies or finely grated lemon or lime zest.

I don't use commercial pectin but prefer to make use of the fall apple bounty; you can use just about any apple. They don't have to be wonderful quality but do cut away any bruised or brown areas first.

Sage and Rosemary Jelly

MAKES APPROXIMATELY 4 4-OUNCE JARS

2 pounds cooking or eating apples
Rind and juice of 2 lemons
A large handful of fresh sage leaves
2–3 sprigs fresh rosemary
Sugar
2 tablespoons chopped sage

Chop the apples roughly (no need to peel or core them) and put them in a large saucepan with the lemon juice and rind as well as the fresh sage and rosemary. Cover with water and bring to a boil; simmer, covered, for at least an hour, by which time the apples should be soft and pulpy. Cool briefly, then carefully tip the mixture into a very large sieve or colander that you have lined with cheesecloth or muslin; set this over a sink or large bucket and leave to drain overnight.

175

The next day measure the apple liquid that has collected in the sink; for every 2½ cups of juice, add 1½ cups of sugar. The cooked apples and herbs can be discarded or added to a compost pile. Return the juice and sugar mixture to the saucepan and heat until boiling. Boil for 10–15 minutes, until the jelly reaches setting point. You can test this by dropping a little of the jelly mixture onto a chilled saucer—cool it and then run your finger through it. If it wrinkles, the mixture is ready.

Cool the jelly, then stir in the fresh chopped sage (and a few rosemary leaves, too, if you like). Place in small glass preserving jars, sterilized according to the manufacturer's instructions. Seal and store in a cool, dark cupboard. The jelly lasts for up to a year but should be kept in the refrigerator once the jar is opened.

Garden Bounty Piccalilli

MAKES AT LEAST 4 ½-PINT JARS

Just the name sounds wonderful! I remember my mom making many, many jars of this delicious sweet and sour chutney in fall; my father loved it and could eat it by the spoonful! It's great with cheese, cold cuts, and vegetables, and it makes a great gift. Apart from the nutritious vegetables, one also receives amazing health-giving benefits from the turmeric, mustard, garlic, and ginger.

- 3 cups small cauliflower florets
- 2 cups peeled baby onions
- 3 carrots, peeled and thinly sliced
- 2–3 red or green peppers, chopped
- 3 small cucumbers, cut into thin slices
- 2 tablespoons salt
- 2 garlic cloves, crushed
- 2 cups apple cider vinegar
- 1½ cups sugar
- 1 tablespoon mustard powder
- 1 tablespoon turmeric
- 1 teaspoon ground ginger

Place the vegetables in a large colander or sieve and stand over the sink or a deep bowl. Sprinkle the salt over them and leave to stand for 4 hours. Drain well. Mix the garlic, vinegar, sugar, and spices in a large saucepan and bring to a boil; simmer for 10 minutes. Add the vegetables and simmer for another 10 minutes. At this point you can also add a tablespoon of celery seeds if you like them.

Divide the hot pickle between sterilized canning jars that you have prepared according to the manufacturer's instructions. Seal, cool, and store. Once the pickle is open, store in the refrigerator. It lasts for several months, although that generally never happens in my experience.

Spicy Pumpkin Chutney

MAKES ABOUT 4 4-OUNCE JARS

A delicious memory of the fall harvest and another wonderful kitchen gift too. Serve this spicy South African chutney with bread, cheeses, cold meats, and as a side dish for roasts and grilled food.

    1 pound fresh pumpkin, peeled
    2 onions, thinly sliced
    3 garlic cloves, crushed
    2 small chillies, sliced
    1 teaspoon salt
    Juice and rind of 1 large lemon
    2 cups apple cider vinegar
    2 tablespoons chopped fresh ginger
    1 cup dark brown sugar
    5 cloves

Cut the pumpkin into small cubes, removing any remaining seeds or stringy pieces. Place the pumpkin in a large bowl and sprinkle the onions, garlic, chillies, and salt over the top. Leave to stand for an hour.

Combine the rest of the ingredients in a saucepan and bring to a boil. Allow to simmer until the sugar has dissolved and the mixture has thickened slightly. Pour the mixture over the pumpkin mixture in the bowl and stir, then return it to the saucepan and cook, covered, over a

low heat, until the pumpkin has softened but is not mushy and the mixture is thick and aromatic.

Spoon the pumpkin chutney into sterilized glass jars, seal according to the manufacturer's instructions, and cool before storing in a cool, dark place. The chutney should be kept in the refrigerator once the jar is opened.

WINTER

Peace & Reflection

inter comes, bringing with her dark, frosty nights and a bare-bones landscape against a cold sky. For those of us who love the warmth and light of summer, this can be a challenging time; in fact, I used to dread the coming of winter and complain about it endlessly until I finally realized two things. Firstly, winter was going to come whether I liked it or not, and there was nothing I could do to change that.

Secondly, and perhaps more powerfully, what I saw as a dead and dreary season was, in fact, anything but. Winter is an essential part of the wonderful cycle of life on this earth, a time when things are stripped back to the basics. Growth continues but in a different and subtle way, just as the cold earth holds the seeds of the new growth in spring. And we can also learn from the many animals who hibernate, retreating to a safe space in order to rest and restore themselves for the coming year.

It's possible to do something similar with our lives, for the winter months offer us a chance to turn inward, rest, and reflect on who we are and what it is that lights us up (and, conversely, what it is that drains our joy and energy). Obviously, the various holidays celebrated over the cold months bring with them not only joy and celebration but also stress and overload as we juggle the many things we have to do, all of which make taking time to explore our own inner being and what we need on a physical, spiritual, and emotional level for wellness and self-care even more crucial.

Using the natural world as a guide and teacher, we can make each winter a gift—something that warms us from within and gives us reason to celebrate, no matter how chilly the weather outside. Harnessing the power of herbs, spices, leaves, and fruit, we can create delicious and healthy ways of supporting ourselves on every level as we grow into a greater sense of peace and self-awareness.

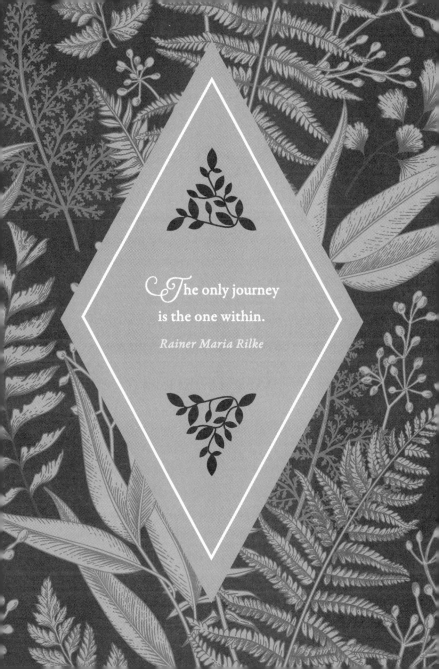

The only journey
is the one within.

Rainer Maria Rilke

HEART NOTES

*L*et us take this new winter season as a beautiful opportunity to discover a little more about ourselves and what brings us peace and serenity in the simplest and most accessible of ways. May we continue to grow just like our mother the earth, who looks cold and frozen at this time of year while under the quiet earth she is alive with the promise of new and wonderful things.

Walking in the Rain

No matter how much we love walking, sometimes the thought of walking on a very cold rainy or snowy day can be challenging, to say the least; it's easier to stay indoors where it's warm and cozy. But we owe it to ourselves to be outside and maintain our connection with the natural world in this quiet season too; this can become a wisdom time as we walk reflectively through the clear winter landscape. There are two simple rules to follow. One, don't think too much about doing it: just go ahead and do it. And two, always dress very warmly. (As the old Swedish saying goes, there's no such thing as bad weather, only bad clothes!)

Realistically, though, we will only enjoy winter walking if we are comfortable in our skins, and that means, in particular, sturdy footwear as well as warm feet, hands, and heads. That way we can focus on the beauty that surrounds us instead of dwelling on physical niggles like frosty toes and cold fingers.

We are probably all familiar with the many health benefits of walking, and in many ways they are increased during wintertime, which is a time when we frequently tend to be more sedentary. Walking tones muscles, improves circulation, and lifts mood, which for many of us is often lower in the dark, cold months. Just being in nature gives us a natural high, a boost on every level; walking quietly, we become more mindful and notice the little moments of beauty around us. Mindfulness and magic are inextricably linked in many ways. We simply cannot find the enchantment inherent in every day unless our eyes and ears and hearts are open. We need to look deeper and beyond in order to grow, discover, and receive.

Some people feel the rain; others just get wet.

Roger Miller

A Book of Being
(Not Doing)

Many of us keep journals and diaries as a way of assembling our goals and plans for the future, and of course there's nothing wrong with that. It can be very helpful and constructive to write down our personal aims and dreams. But in winter's quiet time of reflection and going deeper into heart and soul, I would like to suggest we also keep a small journal about what lights us up from the inside, right here and now, in this moment.

And if for any reason we are struggling to find joy and meaning in the simple reality of our life, this journal can give us a quiet and supportive place to write about these issues and hopefully find some way of moving forward with greater happiness and serenity.

I suggest you find a small, pretty journal or notebook and a suitable pen. At least once a week (or more often if you feel called to do that), set aside some quiet time when you can be sure of being undisturbed—late evening is often a good time. Sit quietly in a peaceful place and light a blue candle (blue is the color traditionally associated with peace and harmony). Some incense is also a good idea and will help lift and clear your mind and mood; I usually choose either of the two traditional favorites, lavender and geranium.

Allow your mind to relax and be open; give yourself time to think about what it is you truly need in order to be peaceful and heal from any stress, anxiety, or pressure you are feeling in your everyday life. If you find this difficult, simply breathe slowly in and out. After a little while, you will start to feel a little clearer and more relaxed, and answers will come.

Write what you are feeling in your journal or notebook as the thoughts and ideas occur to you. There's no need to censor yourself; this is a safe and protected space. When you have finished writing for the day, sign your name and date the page. Then, holding the journal, blow out the candle and incense, and quietly say the following words:

I am here, in this moment.

I am at peace and so I will remain.

Life is offering me all good things and gifts,
and I simply need to be present
with an open and trusting heart.

I am peace. All is good.

And so it is.

Smudging:
The Ancient Gift of Plant and Fire

Smudging is also known as "smoke bowl blessing," a ritual of purification that drives away negative forces while restoring balance, clarity, and peace. Although generally seen as being a Native North American tradition, similar forms of cleansing have been used throughout the world for many centuries by such cultures as diverse as the Chinese, Zulu, and Maori.

In the winter months, when we seek to purify and calm our minds and hearts, this seems like a particularly appropriate ritual whether you choose to use it for yourself, your home, or for others. Originally the smudging was done using a special bowl, although later it also became common practice to use a smudge stick of dried herbs and wood. I still prefer to use a bowl and have a particularly beautiful large shell, which was a gift from a friend who had been to Hawaii; the energy of this shell seems to tap into the intent of the smudging ritual perfectly.

There are several herbs widely used in smudge ceremonies, with the chief of them being sage (which imparts wisdom, healing, and protection) or sweetgrass and lavender (for loving, peaceful energy). In addition, during the ceremony you can also burn incense, light candles, or add lavender oil to a diffuser.

Simple smudge mixtures:

SAGE, SWEETGRASS, AND JUNIPER: to cleanse and
protect

SAGE, LAVENDER, AND CEDAR: for emotional clarity
and healing body/spirit

ROSEMARY, JUNIPER, AND CEDAR: clarity of
thinking

SAGE, FRANKINCENSE, AND LAVENDER: opening to
the spirit world, awareness, and divination

Smudging is a particularly powerful form of natural magic, if that is the right word, and a highly effective way of conducting special blessings and ceremonies whether for yourself, other individuals, or larger groups. In the Native North American tradition, it is regarded as essential for shifting energy and focus between the world of current physical reality and the unseen world of the spirits.

Basically, you gather the herbs, resins, and other plant material you choose and crumble them together to make a fairly fine mixture. Place a small self-igniting charcoal block in the bottom of your chosen heatproof bowl and light it. When the charcoal has turned grayish-white in color, sprinkle on a few pinches of your herb mixture. It should smoke easily. Keep your mind and heart open and focused, and breathe deeply and slowly as you perform this ritual.

Whether you are smudging yourself, another person, or an area, the process remains the same. Hold the bowl and use a feather to direct the smoke wherever you feel it is needed. If you are smudging a person, start around the head, then slowly bring it down toward the heart area and then down the front of the body. Allow the guided smoke to waft down the back of the body as you breathe deeply and calmly and imagine the smoke bringing with it clarity, peace, and courage. Please be careful doing this if you or the person being smudged is asthmatic or has any kind of breathing difficulties.

To smudge an area or room, simply walk around the perimeter of the area (or around each room), pausing to allow the smoke to waft into each of the four corners. Lavender smudging is particularly appropriate for this since it brings with it such peace and a sense of quiet security.

When you are finished, remove any remaining herb mixture and ensure the charcoal is extinguished. In case of flare-ups, it's always a good idea to keep a jug of water close by. After doing a smudging ceremony, you can say the following blessing:

> *Thank you, smoke and spirits, for the*
> *protection, love, and healing you bring.*
> *Thank you for surrounding us and being with*
> *us as we travel on. Peace is here, and so it is.*

The Four Directions

This simple yet powerful Native American ritual can be used in so many ways: as celebration, growth, and letting go of the past, either as a solitary ceremony or in a group. It is also a natural follow-up to the previous smudging ceremony.

In this ritual we acknowledge the interconnectedness of all life on our earth. We honor both the natural world and ourselves by turning to the four corners—namely north, south, east, and west. It's particularly magical if you do this while holding sage or lavender incense or a smudge stick made with these herbs.

First, turn your body to face the east and say:

> *Spirit of the East, Spirit of Air,*
> *please bless, cleanse, and protect me*
> *and all those in the sacred place.*

Then turn ninety degrees to the south and say:

> *Spirit of the South, Spirit of Fire,*
> *please allow me to see my own*
> *passion, beauty, and strength in every*
> *day I have on this holy earth.*

Then turn ninety degrees to the west and say:

> *Spirit of the West, Spirit of Water,*
> *please bless my dreams and hopes,*
> *and accept my gratitude for your*
> *many and abundant gifts.*

Finally, turn ninety degrees to the north and say:

> *Spirit of the North, Spirit of the Earth,*
> *may you bless and protect this sacred*
> *earth and all who dwell therein*
> *from now on and forever.*

Breathe deeply and slowly, and feel yourself centered and grounded in the moment.

A Winter Feast

Many of the most significant religious and spiritual festivals happen during the winter months, starting with Yule (December 21), Christmas, Hanukkah, New Year, and Candlemas (February 2), also known as Imbolc, which marks the beginning of the end of the winter months and in Native American traditions was known as the cleansing time. Of course, anytime is suitable for a celebration with loved ones and friends who share our lives and earth, as we

need to always embrace the warmth of love, joy, and acceptance, whoever and wherever we are.

However, I would suggest a special feast for February 2—the time when winter is almost past, and we have moved through a time of quiet reflection to a place where we are gently looking forward to new dreams and plans becoming manifest in our lives.

This idea is partially based on one in *The Smudging and Blessings Book* by Jane Alexander. Start by gathering together as darkness begins to fall, with each person holding a candle. Sit quietly in a dark and peaceful room, then slowly stretch the arms up and out, welcoming the coming of new light, warmth, and hope. Gradually light the candles one by one; as they light their candle, each person present can quietly speak of their hopes and dreams for the coming year. When all the candles are lit, stand and form a close circle in a moment of quiet reflection and meditation. Then it's time to share a simple feast of good food and drink, as well as memories of the winter season just past and plans for the coming year.

It's particularly wonderful to use candles and incense infused with juniper, sage, cedar, or frankincense for this.

194

Those who don't
believe in magic
will never find it.

Roald Dahl

Enchanted Feasts Wine Cup

MAKES 8 SMALL FESTIVE CUPS

This is a delicious and celebratory drink to share at a midwinter feast and is a version of traditional mulled wine. Simply pour a bottle of good red wine into a large pan, then add 1 thinly sliced orange, ½ cup brown sugar, 1 cinnamon stick, 4 cloves, 2 bay leaves, and 1 teaspoon grated nutmeg. Simmer very gently until the sugar has dissolved, then cool slightly and strain into heatproof glasses or cups. Float a thin slice of orange in each glass and add a cinnamon stick on the side.

Essential Oils for Healing the Heart

In the winter, as we have noted, there are new challenges, and not all of them are related to the cold weather! It's a simple fact that winter and the holidays often bring up a lot of painful and unresolved issues for many of us; sadly, there is often an increase in depression, panic, insomnia, and anxiety-related issues at this time of year, and the darkness may also play a part for those of us who are affected by seasonal changes.

Obviously it is important to seek help if one is really experiencing major problems in this area, both medically and with supportive counseling or therapy, but on a day-

to-day basis, using certain essential oils can make a hugely positive difference to our mood and happiness.

These oils can be used in various ways: added to massage oils or oils for the bath, used in diffusers, oil burners, or incense, or made into pillow sprays (for peaceful nights) or calming balms to carry along during the day and apply when needed. (There are recipe ideas for all of these in this book.) Or, quite simply, just place a few drops of your chosen essential oil onto a tissue or handkerchief and inhale the aroma as often as you need to.

Some oils to use:

DEPRESSION: chamomile, jasmine, lavender, melissa, neroli, sandalwood, ylang-ylang

GRIEF: bergamot, frankincense, melissa, neroli, rose

INSOMNIA: chamomile, clary sage, lavender, vetiver

MENTAL EXHAUSTION: clary sage, juniper, lavender, neroli, orange, rosemary

PANIC ATTACKS: frankincense, lavender, patchouli, ylang-ylang

STRESS AND ANXIETY: chamomile, geranium, grapefuit, jasmine, lemon, rose, sandalwood, vetiver

CREATE

*T*he winter months are the perfect time to create special and enchanted herbal blends, creams, and nurturing products for body, bath, heart, and soul, as well as for a beautiful home. Take this quiet time as a wonderful opportunity to develop your own magical apothecary mixtures and favorite blends. This is also a beautiful way to make gifts that are truly personal and uniquely handmade.

The Essence of Enchantment

For me and many others, essential oils are well named: I consider them to be essential for anyone who wants to live a more natural, healthy, and simply beautiful life. Obviously there is a wide variety of essential oils available, but with time and practice you will discover which aromas are the most appealing to you; our olfactory senses are so unique that what smells absolutely beautiful to one person can smell positively unpleasant to another! There are many,

many different oils on the market, too, and they vary considerably in both cost and quality. A good rule to follow is: if the price is very low or seems too good to be true, the oil is almost certainly less pure and contains synthetic fragrances. Always try to ensure that you are buying a sustainably produced organic oil. It may cost a little more, but in the long run you will have a far better and effective product. Also, since essential oils are used in such small quantities, they last a long time, provided they are stored correctly (in dark glass bottles, in cool cupboards away from direct heat or sunlight); many oils will last for 3–5 years under optimum conditions.

Some herbal recipes may only call for the use of one particular oil, but in many cases you will need to make fragrant blends of different oils according to personal taste and the particular properties of the product you are planning to make. That's where the magic really begins, for there are no real rules, as such, and you can let your imagination go to a large extent. I would suggest, though, starting with simple blends of no more than two to four oils. Make small quantities at first since if you discover you really don't like a particular blend, it's difficult (or impossible) to make changes at that stage. Once you are more confident, you can add up to seven different oils to a blend.

First, place your base or carrier oil in a small glass jar or bowl (sweet almond, coconut, jojoba, and olive are all good ones), then add the oils, drop by drop. If you are happy with a particular fragrance combination, transfer the oil to a small dark glass jar or bottle and mark it very clearly with the ingredients used and the date so you can re-create the blend at a future date if necessary.

As a very simple guideline, fragrance is usually created using different "notes" that, just like a piece of music, work together to create beautiful harmony. The top notes are "green," with fresh and crisp undertones. Middle notes, which form the heart of a fragrance, are generally the floral ones, such as rose, geranium, and lavender. Base notes are rich and often spicy or woody in aroma: think sandalwood or patchouli; they can give the fragrance an underlying depth and strength.

To make blending a little easier, try dividing your essential oils into fragrance families, which will make this process a little easier. As a general rule, aromas tend to work well with others within the same family and also with fragrances in neighboring families, such as citrus with floral, herbaceous with medicinal, and spicy with woody, but it's not a hard and fast rule and is very much a matter of personal preference. (For example, rose and lavender work beautifully with frankincense.)

200

CITRUS OILS: bergamot, citronella, lemon, lemon balm, lemongrass, lemon verbena, orange

FLORAL OILS: geranium, jasmine, lavender, marigold, neroli, rose, violet, ylang-ylang

HERBACEOUS OILS: basil, chamomile, clary sage, fennel, oregano, parsley, thyme

MEDICINAL OILS: camphor, eucalyptus, peppermint, rosemary, sage, tea tree

SPICY OILS: allspice, cinnamon, clove, coriander, cumin, ginger, juniper, vanilla

WOODY OILS: frankincense, myrrh, patchouli, pine, sandalwood, valerian, vetiver

See the Essential Oils for Healing the Heart section on page 196 for ideas of oils to use for stress-related problems.

Winter Hair Rescue Oil

MAKES ENOUGH FOR 4–6 TREATMENTS

Particularly if it is already dry, fine, or damaged in some way, hair can be particularly susceptible to the cold winter winds and artificially heated environments. This oil is very simple to make and use, and it makes a real difference to hair condition. If your hair is on the oily side, it's best not

to use this more than 1–2 times a month, but for dry and damaged hair, it can be used as a weekly treatment.

In a small dark glass bottle, combine 6 tablespoons organic coconut oil (warmed if it has solidified) with 3 drops rosemary and 2 drops each lavender and tea tree essential oils. Shake well and store in a cool place. To use, take about 1 tablespoon of oil and rub it well into your hair, starting at the ends. Cover your head with an old towel and leave the oil on for 20 minutes before shampooing your hair as usual.

Peaceful Alchemy Fragrant Balm

MAKES 3–4 SMALL POTS

This is probably one of my favorite scent combinations, and everyone who tries it falls in love with the fragrance.

In a small glass bowl set over a pan of simmering water, mix together 1½ teaspoons pure beeswax (either grated or pellets) and ¼ cup sweet almond or jojoba oil. Gently melt the mixture without allowing it to boil. Remove from the heat and add 3 drops each lavender, frankincense, and sandalwood essential oils. You can also add the oil from a vitamin E capsule, if you like.

Stir with a wooden stick to combine well; the mixture will start to thicken. Pour the balm into small glass pots or jars and seal well. Keep cool and dry; apply a little balm

to your wrists, throat, or temples when you need to feel peaceful, harmonious, and relaxed. Don't use this balm on very young children.

A Welcoming Home Infusion

At this time of year, we often have more visitors to our homes than usual; we are often giving holiday parties or entertaining guests. Obviously we want our homes to feel truly welcoming so that all who enter may feel happy, relaxed, and comfortable. This simple home herbal infusion can be used in a number of different ways and is a truly magic way of creating a harmonious environment. If the fresh herbs are difficult to come by at this time of year, feel free to substitute dried.

Combine the following in a large saucepan: several large sprigs of rosemary, a handful of lavender stalks and blossoms, a few basil leaves, and a few slices of fresh ginger. Cover with spring or distilled water and bring to a boil. Then remove from the heat, cool, and pour the liquid into a large bottle or jar. Leave to infuse for 7–10 days, shaking the bottle daily. After that time, strain the liquid into a spray bottle and add ½ cup apple cider vinegar and a pinch of sea salt.

You can simply use this infusion as a fragrant room spray, or you can add it to the water when you are cleaning

floors, cupboards, and windows. Alternatively, set a small bowl of the liquid over an oil burner and allow it to simmer, releasing its fragrance into the air.

Bathtime Magic

In my humble opinion, time spent in the bathtub is an absolute necessity and a way of giving oneself permission to simply be in that moment. It's like a mini retreat for the body and the spirit, and for that reason you will find quite a few special bath recipes in this section.

Invigorating Bath Tea

Make a strong herbal infusion by combining 2 tablespoons each dried rosemary and peppermint in a bowl and pouring 2 cups of boiling water over them. Allow to infuse for 10 minutes, then strain out the herbs and let the mixture cool. Stir in 2 tablespoons Epsom salts and 3 drops each tea tree and sandalwood essential oils. Mix well, then add to the warm bathwater and soak luxuriously. This should not be used if your skin is broken, inflamed, or irritated in any way.

Creamy Bath Melts

I have never had much success making bath fizzies or bath bombs, fun though they are; somehow they don't end up the right consistency and either fall apart or don't fizz when added to the bathwater. Then I discovered a recipe for bath melts, which are much simpler to make and deliciously fragrant and moisturizing. I have changed the original recipe a little to make the bath melts a little denser and more stimulating on the skin. Please note that these bath melts should be kept in a cool, dark place—not in a steamy bathroom or they will become too soft! They also tend to make the tub a little slippery after use, so be careful.

In a small glass bowl set over a pan of simmering water, melt together 2 ounces shea butter and 2 ounces cocoa butter. Then stir in 2 tablespoons coconut oil and 10 drops essential oil of your choice. You can use either one oil or a blend of your favorites; I often make a combination of lavender and either rose or geranium, which soothes and enhances well-being. Finally, stir in 1 tablespoon each Epsom salts and baking soda. The mixture should be smooth and thick. Press it into mini soap or candy molds—silicon, preferably—and allow to firm up. To use, simply rub a melt over your body when you are in the tub; the warm water will melt it down.

This recipe makes about 10–15 melts, depending on the size of the molds.

Sweet Dreams Bath Oil

Making bath oil is just about the simplest way to revive and nourish winter dry skin and make it smell gorgeous as well! While you can use any essential oils you love, the ones I have suggested here are particularly grounding, calming, and add a note of sensuality to bath time.

Pour 1½ cups base oil (sweet almond, jojoba, or grapeseed) into a large dark glass bottle. Add 8 drops patchouli and 4 drops each sandalwood and geranium essential oils. Shake the mixture well and store in a cool, dark cupboard. To use, add about ¼ cup of oil to a tub of warm water and stir it around with your hands before bathing. Please do remember that bath oils make the tub a little slippery, so be extra careful when getting in and out.

Cleopatra's Secret Bath Milk

MAKES ABOUT 3 CUPS, OR ENOUGH FOR 6 BATHS

I think the sultry and beautiful Queen of the Nile would have approved of this luxurious bath soak, even if it doesn't contain her favorite asses' milk but is made with rather humble powdered milk. Please use full cream or whole

powdered milk, as the low- or no-fat varieties are not rich enough.

In a bowl, mix together 2 cups full cream or whole milk powder, ¾ cup Epsom salts, and ¼ cup non-iodized sea salt. Add 10 drops frankincense and 5 drops rose essential oils. Stir in ½ teaspoon ground cinnamon. To make the mix look even more luxurious, add a few dried and crumbled rose petals.

Store the bath milk in an airtight container. To use, scoop about ½ cup under running water and allow to dissolve fully before bathing. This bath milk lasts for up to a year.

NURTURE

*B*eautiful though winter is, she's a season that often brings with her quite a few health challenges, chief amongst them respiratory ailments like colds and flu, sore throats, and sinus infections, as well as aching joints and muscles, which are sometimes exacerbated by the chilly weather. And then there's the tendency we all have to overindulge in good food and drink at seasonal celebrations...But nature has the remedy for us to get us through this time in comfort, good health, and grace.

Sage and Sniffles Tea

Another old, time-tested remedy for the misery of colds and flu; drink this and climb straight into bed. It's pretty much guaranteed that you will feel better by the morning. And if you are like my Scottish great-grandmother, you can always add a tablespoon or two of whisky to the tea for even greater healing properties!

Infuse 1 tablespoon dried sage in ½ pint boiling water for 15 minutes, then strain the liquid. Stir in 1 tablespoon raw honey and the juice of ½ a lemon. Pour into a cup and drink.

Chamomile and Peppermint Tisane

Members of the mint family have long been used for digestive upsets like bloating, indigestion, and nausea. When combined with the soothing qualities of chamomile, this makes a simple and effective remedy for times when we have indulged just a little too much!

Combine the contents of one chamomile teabag with 1 teaspoon dried peppermint, then pour over 1 cup boiling water and infuse for 10–15 minutes. Strain into a cup, stir in a little raw honey if desired, and sip the warm tisane slowly.

Juniper Cleansing Mist

With its distinctive fresh fragrance, juniper is an herb with many applications, from physical ailments to improving mood and relieving anxiety. In winter we often find ourselves in environments that are filled with negative or poor energy, partly as a result of winter illnesses such as colds and flu. This simple room mist serves to dispense these unhealthy energies and create a fresh, purified atmosphere.

Pour ½ cup each distilled water and witch hazel into a small spray bottle. Add 8 drops juniper essential oil, 4 drops lemon essential oil, and ¼ teaspoon borax. Shake the bottle to combine (and also shake before each use) and store in a cool place. Dispense the mist around rooms or even the body, avoiding the face.

Eucalyptus and Jasmine Foot Soak

Feet can find winter a bit difficult too, especially if you are used to spending most of your time barefoot or in sandals. Constantly being bundled up in socks and shoes can leave feet hot, tired, and sometimes a bit smelly, too!

This is a really easy recipe that will ease tired, aching feet while at the same time giving you a chance to sit and relax. Simply fill a large bowl with hot (not boiling) water and add ½ cup each baking soda and Epsom salts and 6 drops eucalyptus and 4 drops jasmine essential oils. (Other oils that would work well for this particular use are lavender, rose, juniper, and tea tree.) Let your feet soak in the bowl for at least 25–30 minutes or until the water starts to get cool. Pat your feet dry, rub on a little moisturizing cream, and slip on a pair of light cotton socks.

Facial Anti-Virus Steam

While I admit that this steam will not necessarily protect you from all the nasty cold and flu bugs that might be flying around at this time of year, using it will certainly leave your senses and body refreshed and purified, and that can only be a good thing. As stated before, don't use facial steams if you have breathing problems or asthma, or if the skin of your face is broken, inflamed, or irritated.

Fill a large basin half full with boiling water, then add 10 drops juniper and 5 drops each neroli, bergamot, and lemon essential oils. Wrap your head and neck in a towel, then hold your face about 8 inches above the water for at least 15–20 minutes, until the water starts to cool. Pat your skin dry gently and add a light moisturizer. If you feel a cold coming on or are already suffering the miseries of congestion, this steam will help to ease symptoms.

Pine for Transformation

We are all familiar with the beautiful and majestic pine tree, which really comes into its own during the winter months, but we may be less aware of the truly magical powers this ancient and revered tree possesses. Pine is, of course, one of the Bach flower remedies, and it is used to help us move beyond guilt, despondency, and feelings of both negativity and lack of self-esteem.

During the winter months, when we can all be prone to times of doubt, unworthiness, and feelings of lack within ourselves, pine is a wonderful way of lifting us up, emotionally and spiritually. You can, of course, make your own pine essence using a few handfuls of fresh needles—see the instructions in appendix C.

Other plants and their essential oils that have positive, uplifting, and peaceful properties include sandalwood, neroli, juniper, vetiver, jasmine, ylang-ylang, and sage. Feel free to include them in any of the health or beauty recipes given in this book.

Healing Hands Herbal Elixir

This simple-to-make healing elixir should have a place in every herbal apothecary; it can be rubbed on sore or irritated skin or a few drops added to the bathtub.

Place 3 tablespoons base oil (jojoba or sweet almond) in a small dark glass bottle; add 5 drops thyme and 3 drops each lemon and neroli essential oils. Shake well and store in a cool, dark cupboard. Shake well before use; lasts up to a year.

Simple Ways to Nurture Your Spirit in Winter

In winter we need light and warmth, both internal and external, to compensate for the dark and cold. It goes without saying that warm clothes and shoes and cozy houses are a necessity, but we can also add beautiful light to our lives by burning fragranced candles or oil lamps night and day (following the usual safety precautions, obviously, as burning down the house is not conducive to a happy winter season).

- As I have said before, I am something of a bath fanatic, and never more so than in winter. Use any of the suggestions in this book or create your own bath blends of oils and salts to make a unique ritual that will both relax and empower you.

- Spend at least half an hour outside every day, no matter what the weather. Breathe in the chilly air and watch the changing moods of the winter sky. If snow has fallen, tap into your inner child and make snow angels or a creative snowman.

- Fill your kitchen with the good aromas of simmering soups and stews enhanced with lots of herbs for health and flavor. Use spices to create baked treats and warming winter drinks. Make dried herb and flower mixes and use them to stitch up little herbal bags or dream pillows (or buy little cotton or gauze bags and use those, simply using pretty ribbons to tie them up with).

- Let go of the busyness that is so prevalent over the holiday season. Simplify your traditions and entertaining wherever possible. You don't need to prepare a nine-course feast simply because you have done so in the past; similarly, if you give and receive gifts over this time, limit the number and expense. The heart is what matters, not the money spent or lavishness of the offering.

- Take time to reflect on the year that is waning and your own personal journey. Yes, there will be things we regret and things left undone, but just like our beautiful earth we have the opportunity to start and begin afresh with new direction and purpose. This is a good time for creating a vision board, perhaps using insights from our journals, that will guide us forward into the new year with clarity and confidence.

- ◆ Gather some beautiful fallen branches and pine cones, and arrange them in a bowl or basket. Reflect on the magic that fills the earth and the magic in each and every plant, tree, and living creature. *We* are magic, and in this icy season, as in every season, we should honor and celebrate all beings, all life.

GROW

*T*he winter garden is a quieter one, seemingly resting under a layer of frosty earth, but, in reality, continuing to enchant and hold the promise of new life and growth yet to come; we just have to have the open hearts to see it. And I hope you are still able to gather fresh herbs, either from your garden or your indoor kitchen garden! Nothing is more life-affirming than being able to continue harvesting and enjoying the simple gifts of the earth year-round, especially on the short, dark days.

Some Herbs to Know

The herbs I have included here are all earthy herbs that add character, warmth, and color to all kinds of winter dishes, as well as numerous healing properties.

Rosemary (Rosmarinus officianalis)

This is probably one of the best known and loved herbs, a woody evergreen perennial that has its place in every

garden. As a plant from the Mediterranean, it likes lots of light and well-drained soil; however, it will continue to grow even through the winter months if it is protected from frost. Some species of rosemary—the smaller spreading varieties—are ideal for growing in containers or hanging baskets.

Few of us can be unfamiliar with rosemary's clear, uplifting fragrance. Valued medicinally for centuries for its antiseptic, cooling, and anti-inflammatory properties, it also has many psychological benefits, which include helping with memory and focus as well as helping us feel revived and energetic when our bodies and spirits are low and debilitated. Rosemary essential oil should be a part of every herbal alchemist's toolkit!

Of course, rosemary is good for remembrance, as the old saying goes, and it is certainly helpful in aiding memory and helping us focus. A few sprigs of rosemary added to a facial steam or floating in a warm tub of water will not only soothe you physically but also boost your imagination and help you move forward creatively and emotionally.

Rosemary is also used widely in the kitchen, although this herb should always be added with restraint since its powerful aromatic oils can overpower all other flavors. Rosemary is traditionally paired with lamb and often chicken; it can be used with fish, although it can be too

strong for delicate whitefish so ideally should be combined with stronger oily fish. I love a little finely snipped rosemary sprinkled on bread and other savory or sweet baked goods—just always remember that less is more.

Parsley (Petroselinum crispum)

Again, probably one of the most widely recognized and used herbs in the world, parsley is extremely versatile, as all parts of the plant can be used: leaf, stem, root, and seed. It's a hardy biennial herb and can be sown successively through spring and summer to ensure a continuous supply into the cooler months. It should be planted in lightly shaded spots with rich, well-drained soil and trimmed regularly to ensure plenty of healthy growth. It also makes a good container herb and as such can be a valuable part of an indoor herb garden.

The two most commonly available varieties are curly parsley and flat-leafed parsley, a Mediterranean variety with a stronger flavor. It's an excellent herb for digestion, being anti-flatulent and able to ease bloating; it has more vitamin C than oranges, and it also contains high levels of calcium, iron, and potassium. It's used as a diuretic and for urinary complaints, and with its antibacterial action, it can protect against illness and help the body detox.

Parsley is a go-to herb in many kitchens, whether added to salads and cold dishes or used in soups and sauces. I prefer to use fresh parsley when possible since I find the dried has considerably less flavor. In general, it works better to add fresh parsley towards the end of the cooking process; otherwise it loses both color and taste.

Parsley essential oil (which is made from the seeds of the plant) is helpful for calming the mind, easing fears, and helping us feel better able to cope with difficulties we may be experiencing in life. You can also use infusions of the leaves, seeds, and roots to help with these issues.

Oregano (Origanum vulgare)

There are many varieties of this vibrant herb, which is actually a close cousin of marjoram, only a little more feisty in flavor. It's both an annual and perennial (depending on variety) and likes well-drained soil and plenty of sunshine. They are very easy herbs to grow but do need quite vigorous trimming back sometimes to ensure they don't become leggy or straggly. Oregano grows well in containers and window boxes as long as the soil is good and they are not overwatered.

Oregano contains high levels of the chemical thymol, which is powerfully antifungal and thus very helpful in many herbal preparations for treating problems such as

fungal infections, fevers, throat issues, and viral infections. If you are having problems with memory loss or lack of concentration, particularly as a result of aging, oregano can be of great help. And for those of us (most of us, I would imagine) who sometimes feel stressed and unable to relax, it's a good calming herb; it's also known as a natural antidepressant, helping lift the mood and ease fears of various kinds.

Oregano and marjoram have been used in the hearty cooking of the Greeks and other countries bordering the Mediterranean for centuries, and with good reason. Oregano, in particular, teams up beautifully with red meat such as lamb or venison, chicken, eggs, and tomatoes. The dried version of the herb is as aromatic as the fresh, so it's a good idea to harvest lots of the fresh leaves in summer to ensure a steady supply over the winter months.

The essential oil is best used in a diffuser or added in very limited amounts to natural products such as room mists or herbal handwashes. It should be used well diluted in base oil and never used during pregnancy or breastfeeding or on young children.

Cinnamon

A very familiar spice, warming and comforting, and most well known to most of us for its use in the kitchen, particularly in spice mixtures and for baking. Cinnamon

also is available as an essential oil, created from the bark and leaves of the plant, and is an uplifting and energizing scent, especially when used in diffusers and room sprays. (Please note that it should always be well diluted.) It is used, in very small quantities, in some beauty preparations, too. This antiseptic and warming spice can be good for sore, painful joints and is helpful for digestive problems.

Sandalwood

This tree, a native of India, has been used in both Indian and Chinese medicine for hundreds of years and is now seriously endangered, so it's very important to seek out sandalwood oil that has been responsibly and sustainably harvested. Quite apart from its rich and spicy aroma, sandalwood has anti-inflammatory and antiseptic properties, and as a decongestant it is helpful for respiratory problems. It restores vitality and can ease depression or aid with insomnia. It's very widely used for incense and other fragrant products, as well as in natural skin preparations, where it helps to balance oily skin as well as treat skin that is blemished, sore, or irritated.

Frankincense

This fragrant tree is a native of North Africa and the Middle East. Created from resinous tree sap, the essential

221

oil has been widely used in religious and spiritual ceremonies and is celebrated for its ability to restore positivity and bring us into a more peaceful, meditative state of mind. Naturally calming, it is an analgesic and anti-inflammatory spice, good when used for conditions like arthritis and rheumatism; frankincense also is helpful for coughs, colds, and bronchitis. As a beauty treatment, it's an excellent facial toner, especially for mature or blemished skins. The wonderful aroma is particularly lovely when used in diffusers, incense, candles, or added to massage oils; I would never be without a bottle of this traditional essential oil.

Vanilla

Probably one of the most familiar scents to many of us, vanilla is generally seen more as a flavoring for baked goods and desserts, but in recent years it has started to be used in aromatherapy treatments and beauty products too. It's a fairly heavy and intense scent, as we all know, so should generally be used in moderation, otherwise it tends to overpower other fragrances. The essential oil of vanilla is soothing and calming for rough, dry, or damaged skin. Vanillin, the main aromatic chemical found in vanilla pods, has pain-relieving properties and a mild antibacterial effect. If you are feeling anxious or negative, this delightful scent will help to improve and lift your mood—maybe

222

that's why we find the scent of baked goods so delicious! The oil can be added to hair treatments or to a diffuser or oil burner. It's also easy to make your own vanilla extract for use in cooking and baking. Just place a few dried vanilla pods in a glass bottle and cover with vodka. Leave to stand for a couple of weeks, shaking frequently, then strain out the pods—infinitely better than the nasty chemical-laden vanilla essence so frequently found in food markets.

Feed the Birds

I am fortunate enough to live surrounded by many, many birds who are frequent and very welcome visitors to my deck, where I leave food out for them several times a day. To me and many others, these little feathered creatures are truly a gift from Mother Earth: in fact, in some cultures they are considered to be the representation of angels, sent as messengers from heaven. In winter, though, birds and other wildlife sometimes struggle to find adequate or suitable food to sustain them, so creating a feeding station at the coldest times of the year is a wonderful way to support these amazing gifts from nature that bring us constant messages of hope, magic, and cheer.

A particularly nice way to feed birds in the winter is to create seed cakes. I remember my mom making these every winter and then suspending them from the tree branches

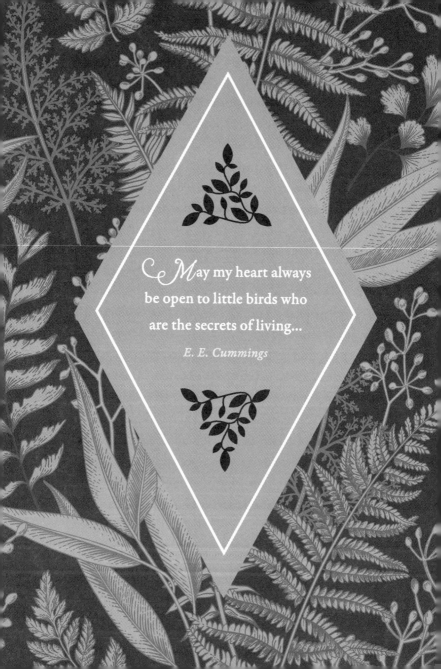

May my heart always
be open to little birds who
are the secrets of living...

E. E. Cummings

above the bird table. She melted lard, then stirred in an assortment of different bird seeds and sometimes small nuts to make a thick mixture. Sometimes she would press the mixture into popsicle molds to get hard, or alternatively she used the scooped-out hollows of an orange as a pretty mold. Whatever you choose, your little feathered visitors will thank you every day in the frosty months.

Also, remember that if the ground is frozen hard, birds will have difficulty accessing fresh water, so place a few small dishes of water outside in the morning. Fruit is also hydrating, so apple or orange halves can be left on the bird table too.

If you have other small wildlife that visit your garden, you might want to consider leaving food for them, too— do a little research on the wildlife in your area to ensure you are giving them healthy and appropriate foods.

Blessings from the Garden

A few years ago, I started a "blessings from the garden" jar; every day I would write something down I had seen in the garden or on my walks, something that had touched my heart or lifted me up emotionally. It might be a flower, a bird, even a heart-shaped pebble or the sound of leaves in a soft wind. I wrote on small pieces of natural or handmade paper, then placed these pieces in a beautiful old jar

225

together with a few small feathers, stones, and dried rose-buds. This jar became very special to me, and ultimately I ended up using some of the images and words I had collected to create an illustrated line of small inspiration cards.

This is, I think, a lovely idea for anyone who wants to create garden enchantment in both their surroundings and their lives. Of course one can keep a garden journal—in fact, I encourage you to do so—but somehow the small affirmations and images on little cards can truly be an everyday touchstone for gratitude and awakening.

Someone asked me, not long ago, how to create a magic garden. There is no secret to this; it's very simple. It starts with the plants and the earth, water, sunshine. Plants, just like us, need basic things like food, moisture, and light; they also need love, companionship, and nurturing. So love your plants and talk to them too; it doesn't matter if people think you're crazy! It's important to find out if the growing conditions where you live are suitable for a particular plant, but other than that, break the rules in a gentle way. Do what looks beautiful and feels right for you—it's your green space, after all.

A magic garden can take you on a journey to a better, more peaceful and abundant life, one in which you and your plants can grow in beauty, grace, and health. Nature

226

is our greatest and best teacher, so we need to learn from her and then extend that gift all around us in love and gratitude.

TASTE

*J*n winter the kitchen can truly become the enchanted heart of the home; it's a place of nurture, comfort, and delicious tastes that supports us both physically and emotionally on the coldest and darkest days of the year. Although some of our herbal choices may be limited in this season—for example, we may have to use more dried herbs if fresh are no longer available—this is no barrier in creating truly magic meals to share and savor.

Scarborough Fair Chicken Broth

SERVES 4–6

This is such a classic winter broth, with truly wonderful life-affirming properties and taste. In this case, I would suggest using fresh herbs if possible, but if not, simply create a bouquet garni by placing 1 tablespoon of each of the dried herbs in the center of a square of muslin, then gathering it up and tying it firmly with string before adding it to the

chicken pot. Otherwise, tie together a few sprigs each of parsley, sage, rosemary, and thyme (and a few bay leaves, if you like) and use as indicated in the recipe.

1 whole fresh chicken, at least 2 pounds
2 large onions, peeled and sliced
3 carrots, peeled and cut into chunks
2 stalks celery, thinly sliced
2 garlic cloves, crushed
1 tablespoon fresh lemon juice
½ cup dry white wine
Fresh or dried herbs, as above
Salt and pepper to taste
Chopped fresh parsley

Place the chicken in a large pot. Add the onions, carrots, celery and garlic, then pour in the lemon juice and wine. Add the fresh or dried herbs and enough water to cover the chicken completely. Cover the pot, bring to a boil, and simmer gently for 1–1½ hours, until the chicken is cooked and tender. Skim off any white scum that rises to the top of the pot.

Lift out the chicken and place it on a board to cool. Discard the herbs. Remove the skin, bones, and fat from the chicken, and chop the meat into small chunks or slices. Return the chicken meat to the broth/vegetables, and add salt and pepper to your taste. Bring to a boil again and serve

piping hot in soup bowls, making sure there are plenty of both vegetables and chicken pieces in each bowl. Sprinkle with extra chopped parsley before dishing up.

Oregano and Olive Flatbread

MAKES 4–6 SERVINGS

Winter is the perfect time for making baked goods, in particular bread, as it represents comfort and tradition in this cozy season. I love making flatbreads with herbs; they are always popular and pair up well with winter soups and casseroles. Oregano is a favorite herb of mine, but you could swap it out with, for example, basil, rosemary, or thyme. For this bread, you can use either fresh or dried herbs; simply reduce the quantity if using dried.

> 1 ounce active dried yeast
> Pinch of sugar
> 4½ cups flour, divided
> 2 tablespoons olive oil
> 3 tablespoons dry white wine
> A large handful of fresh oregano leaves, chopped
> 2 tablespoons pitted black olives, chopped
> Freshly ground sea salt crystals

Combine the yeast and sugar in a large bowl, and add a little warm water to make a smooth paste. Sprinkle in approximately half of the flour and mix to form a dough. Then add the olive oil and wine and knead until you have a soft but manageable dough. Place the dough in a bowl, cover, and leave in a warm place until it has doubled in size, about 1 hour.

Preheat the oven to 400° F and grease a large baking sheet very well. Punch the dough down, then press onto the baking sheet—it should be fairly thin. Leave to rise again for half an hour. Sprinkle with oregano and olives and dust with sea salt. Bake for 20 minutes, until the bread is slightly risen and golden brown; cool briefly in the pan and then serve warm, cut into squares.

Roast Duck
with Ginger, Orange, and Thyme

SERVES 4–6

This is such a celebration dish and perfect for a special winter feast. The tastes are traditional (orange has always been associated with duck) and yet also a little bit different, with the addition of different herbs and spices. Serve this with love in your heart as a truly special and festive meal for dark winter days.

1 or 2 ducks (3–4 pounds in total)

Oil, salt, and pepper to taste

1 large orange

⅓ cup brandy

3 tablespoons honey

1 tablespoon fresh chopped ginger

1 tablespoon dried thyme

¾ cup chicken broth

Cornstarch or flour

A handful of fresh chopped scallions

Preheat the oven to 350° F. Place the duck(s) in a large roasting pan, rub with a little oil, salt, and pepper, and roast for 1 hour, until they are starting to look golden brown. (Pour off any fat that has collected and save it for roasting potatoes.) In a bowl, combine the juice of the orange (keep the skin), brandy, honey, ginger, and thyme. Pour this over the ducks and continue roasting until they are done and the skin is crisp.

Remove the ducks and keep warm. Add the chicken broth to the juices in the pan, bring up to a simmer, and thicken with a little cornstarch or flour if the juice seems thin. Arrange the ducks on a serving platter—I like to cut them up into portions first—then pour over the spicy gravy and add the reserved orange rind, cut into thin strips. Finally, sprinkle with chopped scallions and serve with rice or roast vegetables.

232

Stir-Fry Brussels Sprouts
with Bacon, Pecans, and Garlic

SERVES 4

Even people who say they don't like Brussels sprouts usually enjoy this dish; you can also make it with baby spinach leaves, but in that case you won't need to cook the spinach first.

> **1 pound fresh Brussels sprouts**
> **1 cup chicken or vegetable broth**
> **4 ounces smoked lean bacon**
> **1 garlic clove, crushed**
> **½ cup pecans**
> **Olive oil**
> **½ teaspoon nutmeg**
> **Salt and pepper to taste**

Trim away any damaged parts of the sprouts, then boil them in the chicken or vegetable broth until they are just tender but not mushy. Allow to cool briefly.

Cut the bacon into small pieces or strips, and fry together with the garlic in a large pan until the bacon is fairly crisp. Chop the pecans coarsely. Add a little olive oil to the bacon mixture and stir in the nutmeg, cooked sprouts, and pecans. Cook, stirring for a few minutes, until the sprouts are heated through, then serve while hot.

Peach and Coriander Cobbler

SERVES 6–8

This simple and warming winter dessert always gets good reviews. The ground coriander adds a delicious flavor note to this traditional dessert, which can also be made with apples, pears, or plums.

4 cups sliced peaches, fresh or canned

¼ cup brown sugar

1 teaspoon ground coriander

½ teaspoon ground cinnamon

1 cup sugar

1½ cups flour

1 teaspoon baking powder

½ cup shredded coconut

2 eggs

¼ cup soft butter

Preheat oven to 350° F. Grease a 9 × 13-inch deep baking pan well. Spread the peaches in the baking pan and sprinkle with the brown sugar, coriander, and cinnamon. In a large bowl combine the sugar, flour, baking powder, and coconut. Stir in the eggs and butter and beat well until a soft, smooth dough is formed. Spoon the dough evenly over the peaches and bake until the topping is golden brown. Serve warm with whipped cream, vanilla ice cream, or custard sauce.

234

The Winter Herbal Pantry

Red Onion and Thyme Marmalade

MAKES 4–6 SMALL JARS

So much more delicious than it sounds, this marmalade is a wonderful addition to your winter pantry. It goes well with cheese, meat, breads, and vegetables—just about anything, in fact. A jar of this also makes a wonderful gift.

1 pound peeled and thinly sliced red onions
1 tablespoon dried thyme
Olive oil
Salt and pepper to taste
¾ cup sugar
½ cup red wine vinegar
1 cup red wine

Fry the onions and thyme in a little olive oil until the onions are soft and transparent. Add salt and pepper to taste, then stir in the sugar, red wine vinegar, and red wine, cover the pot, and continue cooking for at least 30–45 minutes or until the mixture is thick. Pour into small, sterilized jars, seal, and cool. Once a jar has been opened, it should be kept in the refrigerator.

Orange Spice Liqueur

MAKES ABOUT 4 CUPS

This is an old South African recipe that needs to be planned well in advance because of all the steps involved. The original liqueur was made with tangerines, and if you can get hold of them, use three or four tangerines instead of the oranges. This spicy liqueur is lovely as a post-dinner drink or added to sauces for desserts.

2 oranges
½ teaspoon nutmeg
5 cloves
1 cinnamon stick
3 cups brandy
1 cup sugar
1 cup water

Peel the oranges, cut the skin into strips, and leave to dry for at least 10 days. Then place the crumbled, dried orange peel in a large jar together with the spices and pour 3 cups brandy over them. Cover the jar and leave to stand in a cool place for at least a month, shaking the bottle well every day.

After that, strain the mixture, keeping the liquid and discarding the orange peel and spices. In a saucepan bring the sugar and water to boil and cook until a thick syrup is formed. Cool and mix the syrup very well with the brandy liquid. Cover and leave for a few weeks for the flavors to develop before pouring the liqueur into small bottles and capping tightly. Use within a year.

CONCLUSION

In the Talmud, the ancient book of Jewish law, it is said every plant has an angel bending over it, whispering "grow, grow..." I believe this to be true—and I also believe *we* are intended for growth in the most simple and natural ways. It's something we can all choose, every day: choose joy, choose abundance, choose the magic.

Offered with blessings and love,

Gail

APPENDIX A

Guide to Basic Ingredients

This is a brief guide to some of the other ingredients used to create magical health and beauty recipes in this book. Some of them you may already have in your kitchen or bathroom, while others are generally easily obtainable in stores or online. This list does not include essential oils, herbs, and so on, which are discussed at length in the different seasonal sections.

ALMOND OIL (SWEET): An excellent base oil for creating natural beauty and aromatherapy products, this is a light golden oil with richly moisturizing properties that can be used for all skin types.

APPLE CIDER VINEGAR: Preferably organic, this vinegar is an excellent natural astringent with refreshing and soothing properties, suitable for most skin types except very dry or sensitive skins.

BAKING SODA (SODIUM BICARBONATE): A white, odorless powder with softening and soothing properties. It's particularly suitable for use in natural bath salts and soaks, and is good at relieving skin irritation and itching.

BEESWAX: Use the best quality unrefined beeswax you can find in your beauty balms and other creations. It can be bought in solid blocks and then grated (which is sometimes quite difficult), so I prefer to use the small beeswax pellets, which are easier to both measure and melt. Beeswax brings its own unique properties and a gentle aroma to natural products. Please don't use synthetic waxes, which are refined and contain chemicals that defeat the purpose of creating natural products.

BENZOIN TINCTURE: A natural (and old) preservative that is used in very small quantities; its old name is friar's balsam. It does contain iodine, which can be an allergen for some people.

242

Borax (Sodium Borate): There is something of a controversy about the safety of using borax, but I have used it for some time and haven't experienced any problems with it. It is a natural crystalline mineral that functions as an emulsifier (binding together oils and water) and a texturizer. It's also a natural preservative and helps to soften hard water. To be on the safe side, it should never be taken internally, and be careful about getting it on or in your eyes. If you have any type of allergic reaction to chemicals, I would also suggest using gloves when working with borax.

Cocoa Butter: Chocolate, but not as we know it, although it does have a wonderful chocolate aroma! Actually, this is a butter derived from the cocoa bean, and it is beautifully creamy and soothing on the skin, making it an excellent choice for lotions, body butters, and lip salves. It hardens at room temperature but melts with the warmth of the skin, and it helps make beauty products that are thick and creamy in consistency.

Coconut Oil: Naturally rich and creamy, with a wonderful tropical aroma, coconut oil has a multitude of uses in making natural body and beauty products. It's particularly good for dry, sun-damaged skins and also makes a wonderful hair conditioner. Use organically grown coconut oil wherever possible; it becomes solid at room temperature but can quickly be restored to its liquid state by placing the jar or bottle in a bowl of warm water.

Epsom Salts (Magnesium Sulfate): Another natural mineral salt with excellent pain-relieving and anti-inflammatory properties. It's good for using in bath salts and blends, and can also be used to relieve painful, aching joints. It's often combined with both baking soda and sea salt in products; however, it is fairly abrasive so should not be used on dry, broken, or irritated skin.

Glycerin (Vegetable): Lighter than oils but with similar properties, glycerin is a clear, slightly sweet humectant (draws moisture into the skin). It's excellent when added to lotions and body products specifically designed for dry or mature skin. It can be used in place of alcohol when

making herbal tinctures and is also suitable for vegetarians and vegans.

HONEY: Preferably raw and organic, since cheaper honey is often adulterated with syrup and other sweeteners. I love adding a little honey to body and beauty products, both for its subtle sweetness and also soothing and hydrating qualities. Please note that honey should not be used on or given to children under the age of twelve months.

HYDROSOLS (FLOWER WATERS): These fragrant waters are a byproduct of the process of distilling and extracting essential oils. The steam left by these processes contains much of the fragrance and healing properties of the original flower or plant. Hydrosols are wonderful used on their own as refreshing and uplifting body or room sprays or can be added to beauty recipes.

Some commonly available hydrosols include:

Lavender—clean, fresh, and calming

Orange Flower—a happy and uplifting scent

Rose—subtle, warm, and relaxing

Rose Geranium—cooling and invigorating

Rosemary—stimulating and refreshing

JOJOBA OIL: Another base oil for aromatherapy and other products, it's a good alternative to sweet almond oil and has a similar composition to the moisturizing sebum found on our skins. For this reason, it is easily absorbed into the skin without leaving a greasy residue. It's a very long-lasting oil, excellent in bath and massage oil blends, for use as a hair conditioner, and to improve the condition of nails.

LEMON: I could not function if my kitchen did not contain lots and lots of lemons! Lemon is such a bright, sunny fruit, and just like orange is packed with healthy vitamin C. Lemon is also a natural bleach and can be used on hair to lighten it naturally and give it a sun-kissed look; it removes excess oil, too, and has astringent and disinfectant qualities when used in moderation in facial and body products, but be very careful not to get any in your eyes. Lemon can be photosensitizing, so don't use lemon-based products or those containing lemon essential oil before spending time in the sun.

MILK (DRIED): Whole dried milk contains healthy fats and lactic acid—it enriches bath mixes and can be added to skin cleansers. Don't use lowfat or no-fat milk powder; it will not work in the same way. If you are allergic to dairy or prefer not to use it, coconut milk powder can be substituted.

OLIVE OIL: Another base oil, although I find its aroma and general heaviness makes it less suitable than other oils. It can, however, be mixed with a lighter base oil, which still allows its many beneficial healing properties to come through. Unfortunately, it can be difficult to disguise its fragrance in beauty products, so it is best reserved for medicinal applications. Don't use extra virgin olive oil—that should be reserved for cooking, where it truly comes to the fore!

ORANGE: Some of the recipes in this book use fresh or dried orange peel or fresh orange juice; obviously, oranges are full of good things such as vitamin C and also impart a wonderful freshness to natural products of all kinds, especially when added to bath scrubs and body care products.

ROSEHIP OIL: This beautiful oil is derived from the Andean rose hip. It's very high in essential fatty acids and is ideal for use on mature, dry,

or damaged skin; it also helps heal and restore scars and stretch marks. It can be added to facial creams and elixirs, where it has shown amazing results. However, it should not be used on oily or combination skins, where it can actually make them worse.

SEA SALT: This has so many different applications and is also available in different forms. Please use pure non-iodized salt without additives; it's best to use finely ground salt, since the coarser salts are very abrasive on the skin. You can also use pink Himalayan salt, which has similar properties and is a delicate pink color that looks great in scrubs and other bath products. Don't use any salt scrubs on the face; they are too harsh and drying. For this reason, they should also not be used on skin that is overly dry, sensitive, or broken.

SHEA BUTTER: A natural product from the karite tree, it's a soft and creamy colored butter-like product; the scent in its natural form is quite pervasive, so I suggest looking for the white, refined version of this butter, which has the same skin-softening and enriching properties, making

248

it an excellent additive to lotions, creams, and other skincare recipes.

VITAMIN E OIL: Available in capsule form, you will find recipes in this book that suggest the addition of one of these capsules; it's an antioxidant oil helpful in healing and restoring damaged, burnt, or scarred skin. It's also a mild preservative when added to beauty products.

VODKA: This-well known alcoholic drink is used in making tinctures of herbal or flower material. It is also a simple preservative often used in the making of herbal colognes, toners, and similar products. Be sure to use vodka that's 80 or 100 proof, but don't use it on dry, sunburned, or sensitive skin.

WATER: One of the most basic and essential of all ingredients! However, when making herbal or natural beauty products, it's a good idea to use only distilled water or pure bottled spring water since that way you are sure of the purity of the water and that no unwanted chemicals or other undesirables will wind up in your products. If you only have tap water on hand, boil it first, then allow to cool before using.

WITCH HAZEL: This commercially available liquid consists of water mixed with added witch hazel extract. It's an excellent natural toner and cleanser, especially for oily or combination skins.

APPENDIX B

Tools and Other Supplies

Many of the tools and utensils one uses for making herbal and flower preparations are undoubtedly things we already have in our kitchens or bathrooms, but here are some ideas for items that are useful to have. I suggest, however, that any utensils and tools you use for herbal concoctions be kept expressly for that purpose and not also used for food preparation. This prevents cross-contamination and spoilage. It's also important to keep all the equipment you use as clean as possible, dust-free, and dry. When you have finished using anything, wash it in very hot, soapy water and leave it to dry on a sterilized surface.

Suggestions for useful tools for the herbal apothecary include:

- Bowls—lots of bowls, from small to large. Heatproof glass or stainless steel bowls are best, while china or ceramic bowls also can work if heat is not being used. Please never use plastic or aluminium bowls, as they absorb odors or can leach into the product. The same applies to any saucepans you use, which should preferably be only glass or stainless steel.

- A mortar and pestle for grinding herbs and spices. (A spice mill also is helpful and quicker to use.)

- A stick-type blender, small blender, or food processor is handy for making herb pastes and the like.

- Secateurs and good kitchen scissors for harvesting herbs. I also have a wonderful pair of little herb scissors which can be used to strip off small leaves from the stems.

- A good cutting board, either wood or plastic; remember to clean it thoroughly after use, and don't use it for food preparation.

252

- A slow cooker (especially the miniature version) can be used to make oil infusions and so on.

- Double boiler—nice if you have one, but it's not essential. I simply use a small heatproof bowl that fits snugly in the top of a saucepan, and it works well. Just ensure the bottom of the bowl doesn't touch the simmering water.

- I mainly use disposable wooden spoons, popsicle sticks, or chopsticks for stirring mixtures. Particularly if you are using essential oils, they tend to leach into the wood so it's best to discard the stirrers after use.

- Essential oil bottles generally have dropper tops, but a few glass eyedroppers are always useful; just be sure to rinse them in really hot water after use and dry thoroughly.

- A few funnels (stainless steel preferably) for pouring your creations into bottles or jars.

- Fine mesh strainers for straining out infusions and the like; they can be lined with coffee filters, too.

- Glass jars in various sizes with strong lids. It's preferable to use dark glass jars—brown or

blue—as this helps keep herbal products fresh longer, but if you can only find clear glass jars, simply wrap them in dark paper tied on with twine. Sometimes plastic jars may be preferable for safety considerations, particularly in bathrooms or around children. If you want to reuse jars, always ensure they are thoroughly cleaned and dried first.

- Little plastic pots are nice for lip balms, scented balms, and the like, and they can be safely carried in a purse.

APPENDIX C

Making Basic Herbal Preparations

There are a few basic herbal preparations used throughout this book, and since the methods used are generally the same, here are the simple guidelines you can use to also develop your own unique recipes using favorite herbs, oils, and flowers.

Infusions

These are the simplest form of herbal preparation, often used in teas, tisanes, or added to bathwater. Infusions can also form part of specific herbal health or beauty recipes. Place the herbs you need (either fresh or half as much dried) in a glass or china bowl (or teapot), then pour in enough just boiled water to cover the plant material and leave to stand for 10–15 minutes. Strain and drink if using as a tea or tisane or allow to cool before adding to other recipes. Infusions can be sweetened with honey, if the taste is not particularly pleasant, or mixed with fruit juice or other teas such as green, rooibos, or Earl Grey.

Herbal Vinegars

Widely used in the kitchen and for herbal medicines, vinegar is a natural preservative and tonic that also helps extract the flavors and medicinal qualities of herbs and flowers. I could not be without herbal vinegars in my cooking, and I also often add them to various health recipes. Use organic apple cider vinegar if possible, as it has so many of its own wonderful antibiotic, antiseptic, and antifungal properties, and it is exceptionally powerful when mixed with herbs and other healing plants.

To make herbal vinegars, use fresh herbs. To prevent the development of mold, ensure they are very well dried out first. Place the herbs of your choice in a large sterilized glass bottle, then add apple cider vinegar until the herbs are completely covered. Seal the bottle (don't use a metal cap as the vinegar will corrode it) and stand in a cool, dark cupboard for at least 1 month to 6 weeks, shaking the bottle well every couple of days. Strain the vinegar and pour the

liquid into a suitable bottle. Herbal vinegars will last for up to two years provided they are stored correctly. Should any mold develop in the bottle or the vinegar appear discolored or contain floating debris, please discard it and make a fresh batch.

If you are making herbal vinegars purely for culinary purposes, the method is the same as the one detailed above, but you can also use white or red wine vinegar or even (in a pinch) malt vinegar, although I think its strong flavor makes it a little overpowering.

Herbal Honey

These are one of my favorite ways of using the power of herbs and other plants combined with the healing deliciousness of honey, and they are often good enough just to eat by the spoonful on their own. Please note once again that any herbs you use should be totally dry to prevent mold forming on the honey.

Very simple to make, you place either ½ cup fresh or ¼ cup dried herbs in an 8-ounce glass jar and pour in enough raw honey to cover—probably about ¾ of a cup. Cover the jar and leave in a cool, dark place to steep for at least 3 weeks. Then strain out the plant material and store the honey in a sterilized jar, well covered.

Good herbs to use for honeys (depending on your intended application, of course) are garlic, oregano, sage, thyme, turmeric, lavender, lemon balm, fresh ginger, mint, or cinnamon sticks. Honey has many antibacterial and immune-boosting properties, so it can be added to tonics and medicines for colds and respiratory problems. It's also soothing on minor burns and wounds. In the kitchen I love drizzling mint, ginger, or rose petal honey over scones, muffins, and pancakes. Herbal honey also makes a wonderful addition to salad dressings and marinades or can simply be stirred into a cup of tea.

Herbal Syrups

Sweet, like honey, but made using sugars or maple syrup; syrups can be used to flavor drinks and cocktails, desserts, sweet sauces, marinades, and brushed over grilled meat or chicken. You can use white sugar instead of the brown or use agave syrup as a sweetener, too.

Combine 1½ cups fresh or 1 cup dried herbs in a saucepan with 3 cups of water; bring to a boil, then let the mixture simmer for 20 minutes or so until the liquid has reduced by half. Strain out the herbs and add 1 cup brown sugar or maple syrup to the liquid; bring to a boil again, then remove from the heat and stir in ¼ cup brandy, vodka, or apple cider vinegar. Pour the cooled syrup into bottles

or jars, seal well, and store in the refrigerator; the syrup usually lasts for up to 6 months. The alcohol or vinegar acts as a natural preservative and prevents mold forming on the surface of the syrup.

Herb Oils

Herb oils can be made using one of two processes: a cold steeping process or a hot oil infusion. Either way, you will need 1½ cups fresh or 1 cup dried herbs. The herbs must be totally dry, without dew or moisture on their leaves. For simple herbal oil, pack the herbs into a large clean glass jar. Pour oil over the herbs; for culinary purposes I like using light olive, peanut, or safflower oil, while for medicinal purposes you could consider coconut (warmed if it has solidified), sweet almond, or jojoba oil.

The herbs should be totally covered by the oil; leave aside in a cool, dark cupboard for 3–4 weeks, shaking the jar occasionally. After this time, strain the oil through muslin, cheesecloth, or a large coffee filter, discarding the plant material. Store the infused oil in a glass jar or bottle with a tight-fitting lid; it should last for at least a year.

Please note that if mold should develop on the oil, it is best to discard it and make fresh to avoid any possibility of contamination or illness.

A hot oil herbal infusion is made using the same ingredients, but the herbs and oil are placed in the top of a double boiler and left to infuse at a very low heat for at least 60 minutes. Stir the mixture frequently. (You can also use a small slow cooker on its lowest setting for this.) After the oil is completely cool, strain it well and store in glass jars for 1–2 years.

Herbal oils are endlessly versatile in the kitchen and can be used for salad dressings, marinades, stir-fries, sauces, and much more. Herbal oils also have similar properties to essential oils, although they are not nearly as concentrated; as such, they can also be used for massage, bath oils, or added to products such as balms, creams, and ointments.

Herbal Tinctures

Tinctures are one of the most potent and long-lasting ways of preserving the active ingredients found in herbs while accessing the medicinal properties of a particular plant in a very concentrated form. They are generally made with an alcohol base, although this can be replaced by either apple cider vinegar or vegetable glycerin if you prefer not to use alcohol. Place 1 cup dried or 2 cups fresh herbs in a large glass bottle and pour in 1½ cups vodka; you can also use brandy or rum, which helps disguise the taste of more bitter herbs. Seal and leave to steep in a cool, dark place for at

least 2–3 weeks, shaking the mixture frequently. After this time, strain the tincture through cloth, discard the herbs, and store the liquid in small dark glass bottles, clearly labelled and dated. Usually tinctures are taken 3 times a day by adding a few drops to a glass of water. (If the taste isn't great, add a little honey or fruit juice.)

Making Flower Essences

Most of us are familiar with flower essences on some level as they are so widely available now and include flowers from many different parts of the world in addition to the wonderful range originally developed by Dr. Edward Bach in the UK. It's a beautiful way of accessing the unique inherent energies present in not just flowers, but also leaves and other parts of a plant. Flower essences offer us the opportunity to tap into these energies to help us with any blocks or emotional issues we might be experiencing.

For some people, the whole concept of flower essences seems a little too esoteric, but I would encourage everyone to try making their own flower essences at least once, using a particular plant or flower that seems to speak to you in some way. You just have to take the time to be quiet, open your heart, and listen down deep.

Making your own flower essences is both easy and quite magical, for each of us will be instinctively drawn to flowers

or plants that call to our own personal energies. Perhaps you will find these flowers in your own garden, on a walk in the country, or even at the local farmer's market. When making essences you don't need to worry if a plant is edible or even poisonous since flower essences do not carry traces of the original plant.

The first step is to choose flowers or plants that you feel a connection with. On a clear, sunny day (this is very important), fill a large glass bowl with spring water and place it in full sunshine. Gather the flowers and plant material into a flat basket; it's good to handle them as little as possible, so use small scissors or plant shears to cut them gently and drop them into the basket. Then, float the plants on the surface of the water and leave in full sun for at least 2 hours. After this time you can remove the plants, using a twig or something similar to scoop them out. Again, you want to handle them as little as possible so that you don't transfer too much of your own energy into the liquid.

Scatter the plant material at the base of a tree while giving thanks to Mother Earth for her beautiful gifts so freely shared with us. Then pour the water into a large sterilized dark glass bottle until it is half full. Fill the rest of the bottle up to the top with brandy or vodka. You have now created the mother essence. Label and date this bottle. To create flower essence bottles for everyday use, take 4–7 drops of

the mother essence and put them into small 1-ounce dark glass dropper bottles. Fill with your chosen alcohol, label, and date. To use the flower essences, add a few drops to a glass of spring water or directly under the tongue. Flower essences can also be added to a tub of warm bathwater.

To make moon essences, which are basically the same but created under the light of a full moon, see page 95.

RECOMMENDED READING

This is just a short list of the herbal/garden/magic books
I turn to most often for inspiration and information. The
older books can often be found in secondhand bookstores,
your local library, or on Amazon.

Alexander, Jane. *The Smudging and Blessings Book:
Inspirational Rituals to Cleanse and Heal.* New
York: Sterling, 2009. A lovely book that introduces
simple rituals as practiced in various cultures
worldwide.

Ball, Stefan. *Bloom.* London: Vermilion, 2006.
A thoughtful, in-depth introduction to the Bach
flower remedies.

Blackie, Sharon. *The Enchanted Life.* September
     Publishing, 2018. Not an herb book as such, but
     a delightful look at how to live an enchanted life
     every day with the emphasis on nature.

Bloom, Jessi. *Creating Sanctuary.* Portland, OR:
     Timber Press, 2018. One of my absolute favorites,
     full of excellent gardening tips and ideas for
     creating green areas of magic and inspiration.

Bremness, Lesley. *The Complete Book of Herbs.*
     London: Dorling Kindersley, 1998. Lots of lovely
     ideas for different herb gardens and an excellent
     resource for beginners.

Buchman, Dian Dincin. *Feed Your Face.* London:
     Duckworth, 1974. This is an older book (one of
     the first herb books I ever owned), but it's still full
     of practical information if you can track down a
     copy.

Dorling Kindersley, eds. *Essential Oils.* London:
     Dorling Kindersley/Penguin Random House,
     2016. This book, from Neal's Yard Remedies,
     is a comprehensive overview of essential oils,
     aromatherapy, and creating blends.

266

RECOMMENDED READING

Dugan, Ellen. *Garden Witchery: Magick from the Ground Up.* Woodbury, MN: Llewellyn Publications, 2003. Another excellent resource with lots of seasonal gardening information and ideas.

Fewell, Amy K. *The Homesteader's Herbal Companion.* Lanham, MD: Rowman and Littlefield, 2018. An excellent herbal resource, with gardening tips, recipes, and even remedies for pets and livestock. This book makes me want to run away and live in the country!

Griffiths, Jane. *Jane's Delicious Herbs.* Cape Town: Sunbird Books, 2016. This is a South African book, but it's full of information that can be used globally, so it might be worth trying to track down a copy.

Jirsa, Amy. *The Herbal Goddess.* North Adams, MA: Storey Books, 2015. A selection of twelve of the most commonly used herbs and spices and wonderful ways to grow and use them for both physical and emotional purposes.

Little, Kitty. *Kitty Little's Book of Herbal Beauty.* London: Penguin Books, 1980. I've had this book for years and still find it full of good sense and herbal wisdom.

McBride, Kami. *The Herbal Kitchen.* San Francisco: Conari Press, 2010. Full of wonderful recipe and pantry ideas.

Murphy-Hiscock, Arin. *The Green Witch.* MA: Adams Media, 2017. Natural magic explained and simplified.

Nickerson, Brittany Wood. *Recipes from an Herbalist's Kitchen.* North Adams, MA: Storey, 2016. I think if I had to choose, this is probably the one book I would keep—not only for the delicious recipes but for the wealth of general herbal information and insight it contains.

Robertson, Debora. *Gifts from the Garden.* London: Kyle Books, 2012. Great natural garden and gift ideas.

Sullivan, Rebecca. *The Art of the Natural Home.* London: Kyle Books, 2017. A good introduction to living a simpler, greener life.

RECOMMENDED READING

Telesco, Patricia. *A Floral Grimoire.* New York: Kensington Publishing, 2001. How to use flowers for charms, spells, and enchanted rituals.

Toll, Maia. *The Illustrated Herbiary.* North Adams, MA: Storey Books, 2018. A fascinating and bewitching guide to 36 botanicals and the magic and inspiration they have to share with us.

Tourles, Stephanie. *Organic Body Care Recipes.* North Adams, MA: Storey Books, 2007. Recipes for herbal formulas for hair, body, and bath, as well as information about natural ingredients.

Whitehurst, Tess. *The Magic of Flowers.* Woodbury, MN: Llewellyn Publications, 2016. The ultimate guide to 80 flowers and their holistic and therapeutic benefits, including flower essences, essential oils, aromatherapy, and healing rituals.

RECOMMENDED READING